Defining

National

Security

Defining

National

Security

The Nonmilitary Aspects

Joseph J. Romm

COUNCIL ON FOREIGN RELATIONS PRESS

NEW YORK

COUNCIL ON FOREIGN RELATIONS

The Council on Foreign Relations, Inc., is a nonprofit and nonpartisan organization devoted to promoting improved understanding of international affairs through the free exchange of ideas. The Council does not take any position on questions of foreign policy and has no affiliation with, and receives no funding from, the United States government.

All statements of fact and expressions of opinion contained in Council books are the sole responsibility of the author.

If you would like more information about Council publications, please write the Council on Foreign Relations, 58 East 68th Street, New York, NY 10021, or call the Publications Office at (212) 734-0400.

Library of Congress Cataloging-in-Publication Data

Romm, Joseph J.
  Defining national security : the nonmilitary aspects /
Joseph J. Romm
      p.   cm.
  Includes bibliographical references.
  ISBN 0-87609-135-4 : $10.95
  1. United States—Economic policy—1981–   2. National
security—United States.   3. Narcotics, Control of—United
States.   4. Environmental policy—United States.   5. Energy
policy—United States.   I. Title.
HC106.8.R638   1993
338.973—dc20   92–42451
                                                            CIP

93 94 95 96 97 98 EB 10 9 8 7 6 5 4 3 2 1
Cover design: Patrick Vittaco

CONTENTS

FOREWORD

For decades, the term national security has meant—
by and large—military security. That meaning has
increasingly been called into question as the waning
tensions of the Cold War have coincided with rising
concern over a variety of nonmilitary threats to
America's security.

In this study Joseph Romm examines the growing policy debates concerning several of these new
threats: domestic drug use and the international
drug trade; the greenhouse effect and other global
environmental problems; America's growing dependence on imported oil; and America's declining
economic competitiveness. In each case, Romm analyses the implications of these threats to our conception of national security and the tradeoffs
between domestic and foreign policy priorities. He
argues that many of the new national security
threats are interconnected; that energy security is,
for instance, inextricably tied to environmental
and economic security issues. In his summing up
he offers a new definition of national security and
suggests a new national agenda.

This essay is part of the Council's ongoing effort
to explore new dimensions of American security
concerns in the aftermath of the Cold War and offers

a starting point for further research and debate. It was funded by The Pew Charitable Trusts as part of the Council's Project on America's Task in a Changed World.

Peter Tarnoff
President, Council on Foreign Relations

January, 1993

ACKNOWLEDGMENTS

The research and writing of this paper was made possible by funding from the Council on Foreign Relations' Pew Project on America's Task in a Changed World. I am particularly grateful to Patricia Ramsay and Gregory Treverton for their insightful comments, and to Linda Wrigley for her general editorial assistance. I am also obliged to the many people who attended the CFR workshop on this paper and provided comments on early drafts. Special thanks go to Paul Kennedy for chairing the workshop and to Peter Gleick for bringing to bear his expertise on the discussion of environmental security. Lastly I remain indebted to the many scholars across a host of disciplines whose work I have surveyed in this paper.

I

The Concept of National Security

The nineteenth-century English poet Matthew Arnold wrote of "wandering between two worlds, one dead, the other powerless to be born." So we wander today. For 45 years the United States pursued a national security strategy focused on one goal: containing the Soviet Union. But with the collapse of the Soviet Union and the Soviet empire, the doctrine of containment has become a victim of its own success.

As Americans search for a new direction, the debate over what problems constitute a threat to national security has been renewed. Analysts from a variety of fields have identified a host of new threats: the budget and trade deficits, the stagnation of American wages in the face of global economic competition, and the degradation of the environment. Our existing security paradigm is increasingly inadequate to address these problems.

Military security has not vanished as a key element of national security, but it has certainly declined in importance relative to the issues of economic, energy, and environmental security.[1] In any case, an assessment of military security is not the aim of this essay, and it will be discussed only as it relates to the other security issues being discussed (for instance, how environmental degradation might lead to increased military conflict).

This essay will focus on the circumstances that have led analysts and policymakers to identify non-military problems as serious threats to U.S. security, as well as what the scholarly and policy communities have to say about how these problems might fit into a post–Cold War national security paradigm for the United States. Bearing in mind Voltaire's admonition, "if you wish to converse with me, define your terms," terms such as "national security" and "economic security" will be defined as specifically as possible.

Although the phrase "national security" was not widely used until after World War II, Yale undergraduates debated the question, "Does the National Security depend on fostering Domestic Industries?" as far back as the early 1790s.[2] Discussions of America's national interest and foreign policy priorities had an economic component in the 1930s, and one of the arguments advanced prior to 1941 for going to war with Germany and Japan was that doing so would allow the United States to maintain access to foreign markets and avoid industrial strangulation.[3]

Some would trace the modern etymology of the phrase to an August 1945 Senate hearing: "Our national security can only be assured on a very broad and comprehensive front," Navy secretary James Forrestal told the Senate. "I am using the word 'security' here consistently and continuously rather than 'defense.'"[4] Replied Sen. Edwin Johnson, "I like your words 'national security.'" Forrestal apparently had in mind a broader construction of the phrase than his comment suggested, since in the same hearing he said, "The question of national security is not merely a question of the Army and Navy. We have to take into account our whole potential for war, our mines, industry, manpower, research, and all the activities that go into normal civilian life."[5]

While the phrase may have needed explanation in 1945, it had become so widely used by 1947 that the National Security Act, which established, among other things, the National Security Council, did not bother to define the term but left it open to broad (i.e., not purely military) interpretations by stating that "the function of the Council shall be to advise the President with respect to the integration of domestic, foreign, and military policies relating to the national security. . . . "

The definitional problem, and its dangers, was never lost on either the scholarly or political communities. As early as 1950, the political scientist Harold Lasswell noted that "all measures which are proposed in the name of national security do not necessarily contribute to the avowed end. . . . Our greatest security lies in the best balance of all instruments of foreign policy, and hence in the coordinated handling of arms, diplomacy, information, and economics; and in the proper correlation of all measures of foreign and domestic policy."[6] Another eminent political scientist, Arnold Wolfers, in his 1962 essay "National Security as an Ambiguous Symbol," wrote of the phrases "national security" and "national interest":

> They may not mean the same things to different people. They may not have any precise meaning at all. Thus, while appearing to offer guidance and a basis of broad consensus, they may be permitting everyone to label whatever policy he favors with an attractive and possibly deceptive name.[7]

In part, this ambiguity came from the inherent subjectivity in determining the threats to any nation's security. More recently, the British scholar Barry Buzan has argued that a another reason national security remains a "weakly conceptualised, ambiguously defined, but politically powerful concept" is that "for the practitioners of state policy, compelling reasons exist for maintaining its symbolic ambiguity. . . . An undefined notion of national security offers scope for power-maximising strategies to political and military elites, because of the considerable leverage over domestic affairs which can be obtained by invoking it."[8]

In the American case, increased ambiguity derived from the fact that Washington's principal post–World War II national security mission—containing the Soviet Union—was one it was trying to accomplish primarily by nonmilitary means. Although the United States was not faced with the classic national security burden—ensuring its territorial inviolability—as its principal concern, Congress in part justified a major infrastructure bill—the National Defense Highway Act, funding the construction of 40,000 miles of new highways—as a means of rapidly transporting armaments throughout the country in the event of war. Such a broad conception of national security could justify not only massive foreign aid under the Marshall Plan, but also the National Defense Education Act (1958), a post-*Sputnik* bill aimed at developing a generation of American scientists and engineers, and the establishment of the Defense Department's Advanced Research Projects Agency (1958), which would ultimately fund a host of civilian research and development projects.

Representative Moss, chairman of the House subcommittee that considered the original 1967

Freedom of Information Act, complained in 1973, "National security [is] such an ill-defined phrase than no one can give you a definition. . . . In 16 years of chairing the committee . . . I could never find anyone who could give me a definition." William Blair, deputy assistant secretary of state for public affairs, told Congress in 1972, "Our national security today depends on things like balance of payments, economic affairs, foreign assistance. . . . " The *Yale Law Review* noted in 1976: " 'National security' has long been recognized by courts . . . as a notoriously ambiguous and ill-defined phrase."[9]

Various definitions of national security, made before and since that time, only underscore the ambiguity of the concept:

- *Walter Lippmann* (1943): "A nation has security when it does not have to sacrifice its legitimate interests to avoid war, and is able, if challenged, to maintain them by war."

- *National Security Council* (1950s): "To preserve the United States as a free nation with our fundamental institutions and values intact."

- *Arnold Wolfers* (1962): "Security, in an objective sense, measures the absence of threats to acquired values, in a subjective sense, the absence of fear that such values will be attacked."

- *International Encyclopedia of the Social Sciences* (1968): "The ability of a nation to protect its internal values from external threats."

- *Amos Jordan and William Taylor* (1981): "National security, however, has a more extensive meaning than protection from physical harm; it also implies protection, through a variety of means, of vital economic and political interests, the loss of which could threaten fundamental values and the vitality of the state."

- *Charles Maier* (1990): "National security . . . is best defined as the capacity to control those domestic and foreign conditions that the public opinion of a given community believes necessary to enjoy its own self-determination or autonomy, prosperity, and well-being." [10]

Now that the Soviet Union and Warsaw Pact have collapsed, the United States is very secure according to the narrower definitions, such as Lippmann's. Many of the other—broader—definitions, however, would suggest that the United States suffers from extreme insecurity. A definition I will turn to throughout this essay is one that was offered by Richard Ullman in 1983: "A threat to national security is an action or sequence of events that (1) threatens drastically and over a relatively brief span of time to degrade the quality of life for the inhabitants of a state, or (2) threatens significantly to narrow the range of policy choices available to the government of a state or to private nongovernmental entities (persons, groups, corporations) within the state." [11]

Since the end of World War II, there have been two periods in particular that have led to a broadening of the idea of national security. The first occurred in the mid-1970s, which saw the U.S. failure in Vietnam, rising inflation, the growing economic strength of Europe and Japan, and the first oil shock. In a 1974 essay titled "The Legitimate Claims of National Security," Gen. Maxwell Taylor stated that "the most formidable threats to this nation are in the nonmilitary field," including the energy crisis, the population explosion, and "retarded economic growth, higher costs of industrial production, new deficits in international payments, and increased inflation." In his 1977 paper, "Redefining National Security," Lester Brown, the president of the Worldwatch Institute, discussed the energy crisis and such "economic threats to security" as inflation and migration, as well as "food insecurity," and related factors such as deforestation, soil erosion, and the threat of climate modification, including the greenhouse effect.[12]

The second period began in the late 1980s with the waning of the Cold War. In the Spring 1989 issue of *Foreign Affairs*, Jessica Tuchman Mathews, vice president of the World Resources Institute, wrote that global developments suggested the need for broadening the definition of national security "to include resource, environmental, and demographic issues." And in the Winter 1990/91 issue of *Foreign Affairs*, Theodore Moran, director of the Program in International Business Diplomacy at Georgetown University's School of Foreign Service, listed six "primary areas" for U.S. national security policy in the 1990s: "encouraging stability and reform in the Soviet Union, maintaining a cooperative U.S.–Japanese relationship, and avoiding vulnerabilities from the globalization of America's defense industrial base [and] reducing dependence on oil from the Persian Gulf, moderating the impact on the Third World of the prolonged debt crisis, and limiting the damage from the narcotics trade."[13]

This brief overview suggests that U.S. national security has always had a nonmilitary component, that the phrase has never been well defined, and that

if the term national security is not already meaningless, there is a serious risk that it is rapidly becoming so, as every problem the nation faces is
characterized as a threat to its security. The definitional problem seems certain to get worse, since if
security involves broad economic, energy, environmental, and drug-related concerns, the numbers
of those qualified to address security issues will
include not only military and strategic studies
experts, but also economists, business leaders, scientists, ecologists, and health experts. Perhaps it is
true that, as Harold Lasswell wrote in 1950, "There
are no experts on national security. There are only
experts on aspects of the problem."[14]

II

Drug Policy and National Security

In the 1980s, the "war on drugs" became one of the greatest concerns of the American people and the U.S. government, provoking a debate over whether or not America's drug problem is a national security issue that can be solved by military means.

The global illicit drug trade may be as high as $500 billion. America is the world's largest consumer, with 30 million U.S. users spending an estimated $28 billion per year on cocaine, $68 billion on marijuana, and from $10 billion to $12 billion on heroin. Imports account for 80 percent of all illegal drugs and 100 percent of the cocaine and heroin consumed in the United States.[15] The domestic toll resulting from drug use includes the rapid rise in drug-related violent crimes in our nation's inner cities and soaring health care costs, not least from the accelerated spread of AIDS via drug users.

In 1986, President Ronald Reagan signed a secret directive "that identified the illegal traffic as a national security threat and authorised the Department of Defense to engage in numerous antidrug operations." Although many in the Pentagon initially expressed reluctance against participating in the drug war (and some still do), in September 1989 Secretary of Defense Dick Cheney issued a directive stating: "Detecting and countering the production and trafficking of illegal drugs is a high priority national security mission." Cheney's guidelines further asserted: "The Department of Defense will assist in the attack on production of illegal drugs at the source." A February 1992 draft Pentagon report on post–Cold War strategy listed "threats to U.S. society from narcotics trafficking," as one of the interests that the United States retains "pre-eminent responsibility for addressing."[16]

The total cost of Defense Department interdiction activities rose from about $5 million in FY 1982 to $400 million in FY 1987, to $888 million in FY 1990, to $1.2 billion in FY 1991. The Pentagon now has hundreds of soldiers on antidrug operations on the ground in Central and South America, and U.S. aircraft logged more than 37,000 hours there on drug missions in 1991.[17] The drug war has thus become a component of our national security strategy in the traditional sense of providing direction for possible military activity.

Some drug policy analysts are supportive of this foreign policy approach. Scott MacDonald, author of several books on the drug trade, details the dangers of the "drug insurgency nexus" in Latin America, "a marriage of convenience between drug traffickers (narcotraficantes) and leftist revolutionary groups, such as Colombia's M-19 or Peru's Sendero Luminoso (Shining Path)."[18] Others, however, take exception to the notion that the drug problem is one whose solution lies primarily outside the borders of the United States, that drug trafficking is a threat to U.S. security, or that a military-oriented approach is appropriate. As the director of the Center of International Studies at the Universidad de los Andes in Bogota, Juan Tokatlian, wrote of U.S. policy in 1988: "Drug use is considered a malignant phenomenon whose nature is best explained by external factors and variables. . . . Such is the case with the term *drug trafficking*, which suggests the external dimension of the issue: i.e., that the core of the problem is the *traffic in* and transport of drugs, rather than their consumption."

Tokatlian argues that "employing a strategic-military rationale to deal with the drug problem leads, and has led, to an interventionist attitude and policy which places national sovereignty in great jeopardy."[19] Raphael Perl, a specialist in international affairs with the Congressional Research Office, worries about the use of U.S. military forces in antinarcotics operations in other countries:

> An increase in militarization of what is basically a domestic law enforcement problem raises the specter that US aid designed to strengthen the armed forces in their counter-narcotics operations might (1) inadvertently foster abuses of human rights as soldiers are not trained to respect the rights of civilians, and/or (2) could strengthen the military at the expense of civilian government, thus undermining the authority of already beleaguered democratic governments and the very institutions which the US would like to encourage.[20]

Lt. Col. Michael Dziedzic, a tenured professor of political science at the Air Force Academy, argues that "the drug threat, in spite of its severe national security implications, is not inherently a military threat. It is a *criminal activity*. . . . The straightforward application of military firepower to this problem is not likely to be effective."[21] Donald Mabry writes of the "resort to the inappropriate means of a military solution to a civic/social problem."[22] Furthermore, Tokatlian takes issue with the very idea of a "war" on drugs: "The concept of war demands that the predominant instruments should be of a coercive-repressive nature. In this logic, there is no room for the suggestion that demand may be generating the supply. . . . [T]he objective is to enlist the world in a major effort to reduce that supply. The assumption is that a reduced supply would then have the effect of reducing consumption by individuals in the United States." Perl notes, "Of the [U.S. government antidrug] budget proposed for 1991, roughly 71 percent [was] slated to reduce supply (both foreign and domestic) and 29 percent to reduce demand."[23]

Theodore Moran believes the supply-side approach will not work because

> the profitability of the current system is so great that even dramatically improved success in supply-side enforcement (interdiction of production and distribution) will only marginally offset the incentive for generating new sources. The prospect of providing alternative economic opportunities to woo Peruvian, Colombian, and Bolivian peasants away from coca production appears dim when one considers that marijuana has come to be the largest cash crop of California's rich, fertile and irrigated agricultural regions, where alternative opportunities are abundant.[24]

Carlton Turner, President Reagan's director of drug abuse policy, said in 1991, "You can spend the country into bankruptcy and never stop the drugs coming in."[25]

There are clearly problems with the supply-side approach. The General Accounting Office reported in 1991 that the flow of drugs and drug profits from Panama had increased dramatically since the U.S. military removed Gen. Manuel Noriega from power in December 1989.[26] The same number of people used cocaine weekly in the United States in 1991 as in 1989. Recent studies by the General Accounting Office, the State Department, and the Pentagon have concluded that U.S. counternarcotics programs in Central and South America have not been effective.[27] In January 1992, Central Intelligence Agency (CIA) director Robert Gates told the Senate Armed Services Committee that eradication and interdiction measures in source countries "have not measurably reduced supplies, which continue to be more than adequate to meet demand."[28]

Definitional Issues

The drug policy debate raises many issues that will recur throughout this paper. As Waltraud Morales points out in "The War on Drugs: A New US National Security Doctrine?"

> "national security," as defined by defence specialists, first entails defense in its narrowest concept— the protection of a nation's people and territories from physical attack; and second, the more extensive concept of the protection of political and economic interests considered essential by those who exercise political power to the fundamental values and the vitality of the state. In the last three decades, as US policy-makers became increasingly involved in a more interdependent, chaotic and threatening world, the concept became broader still, until foreign and domestic policy almost completely overlapped. Thus "national" security became "globalized" security encompassing not only real or alleged external military and defence concerns, but virtually unlimited interests and "threats" abroad.[29]

As Morales suggests, the question whether the drug issue should be considered a national security problem is related to the larger question raised above: Does the fact that a problem can be approached (though not necessarily solved) through traditional security methods automatically make it a national security problem? If much (if not most) of the source of a problem is domestic rather than foreign, can it still be considered a national security problem?

In the case of drugs, Tokatlian's division of the problem into two parts, international drug trafficking and domestic drug consumption, is definitionally useful. Domestic drug consumption is a societal ill that is not usefully defined as a national security problem. International drug trafficking, insofar as it supports terrorism and threatens the stability of nations that Washington considers to be of strategic importance, does fall within the realm of traditional security problems, although it is not one of the first rank such as nuclear proliferation or the stability of the Persian Gulf. Such a distinction is particularly justifiable since it appears that efforts to destroy or interdict drug supplies will not significantly affect drug use in this country (either because the efforts fail directly or because alternative supplies replace those that are squelched). Drug trafficking should not be seen as the cause of domestic drug consumption and its concomitant problems and, therefore, it should not be viewed as a significant threat to the nation's security.

III

Environmental Security

The call to redefine national security so as to include environmental issues has been made with increasing frequency over the last few years, in part because the waning of the military tensions of the Cold War has coincided with the growing visibility of problems that threaten the "security" of many nations and require international solutions—the hole in the protective ozone layer, deforestation, acid rain, and global warming, among others.

While advocates list any number of environmental problems that might be called environmental security threats, they rarely give a definition of the term "environmental security." Leaving aside the definitional issue for the moment, we can divide environmental security issues into two categories: (1) transnational environmental problems that threaten a nation's security, broadly defined (i.e., problems, such as global warming, that "threaten to significantly degrade the quality of life for the inhabitants of a state") and (2) transnational environmental or resource problems that threaten a nation's security, traditionally defined (for example, those that affect territorial integrity or political stability, such as disputes over scarce water supplies in the Middle East or the question of what to do with refugees fleeing a degraded environment). The interdependent nature of environmental problems, however, means that these categories are not completely distinct. Related to these is a third category, the environmental consequences of warfare. This is not a new issue—the Romans destroyed the fields of Carthage by spreading them with salt—but it is one that has recently received a great deal of attention because of Saddam Hussein's use of oil spills and oil fires as weapons of warfare.[30] The Environmental Modification Convention of 1977 forbids "hostile use of environmental modification techniques having widespread, long-lasting or severe effects as the means of destruction, damage or injury to any other State Party."[31]

Global Environmental Problems

Of all the environmental security threats now being discussed, global climate change has received the most attention in the last few years. This is true for two reasons. First, the discovery in 1985 of a hole over Antarctica in the earth's ozone layer, which protects life from the sun's harmful ultraviolet rays, was, according to the National Academy of Sciences, "the first unmistakable sign of human-induced change in the global environment. . . . Many scientists greeted the news with disbelief. Existing theory simply had not predicted it."[32] Chlorofluorocarbons are the principal cause of ozone depletion. Second, the seven hottest years of the century all occurred in the 1980s (and the ten hottest have all occurred since 1973). Public awareness of climate change became particularly acute in 1988 (which until 1990 was the warmest year on public record), a year of heat waves, fires, floods, drought, and a superhurricane. James Hansen, director of NASA's Goddard

Institute for Space Studies, said he was "99 percent confident" that the warming trend since 1900 was real and that we should accept the idea that the greenhouse effect was responsible.[33] Since then, the national and international scientific communities have reached a broad consensus on global warming, and it is worth reviewing what they have concluded before examining what others have said about the security implications of this phenomenon.

In June 1990, the science working group of the United Nations' Intergovernmental Panel on Climate Change (IPCC) asserted:

> We are certain of the following: . . . emissions result-ing from human activities are substantially increas-ing the atmospheric concentrations of the greenhouse gases: carbon dioxide, methane, chloro-fluorocarbons (CFCs) and nitrous oxide. These in-creases will enhance the greenhouse effect, resulting on average in additional warming of the Earth's surface.[34]

Atmospheric carbon dioxide concentrations have risen roughly 25 percent since preindustrial times. The earth's surface temperature is estimated to have risen between 0.3° C and 0.6° C in the last 100 years. The expected doubling of heat-trapping greenhouse gases over preindustrial levels by the middle of the next century is projected to raise the average tem-perature of the earth between 1° C and 5° C over the next 100 years. This view is shared by the National Academy of Sciences[35] and the IPCC. Although cli-mate modeling is an uncertain science and not all scientists accept these projections, more than 95 percent of the global team of 200 scientists who participated in the IPCC study were in agreement.[36]

The effect of such warming also cannot be known for certain. In part, this is because a warming of 2° to 2.5° C, which is near the middle of the expected range, would make the earth hotter than it has been in the 10,000 years of human civilization, hotter than it has been in 125,000 years, when humans existed in primitive hunter-gatherer communities: there is no historical basis for determining the outcome.[37] The warming is likely to raise sea levels. A one-foot rise (which is in the middle of the expected range) would pose a serious problem for Bangladesh, the Nile Delta, China, Japan, and the Netherlands. One-third of the world's people live within 40 miles of the sea, where the soil is the richest and the land the lowest. As sea levels rise, we may well see millions of environmental refugees. The United States itself has more than half its population living on or near its coasts. Take just one example of what an increase in sea levels could mean: a three-foot sea rise would double the worst-case flooding of Charleston, South Carolina.[38]

A 1991 National Academy of Sciences study warns of the degradation of agriculture, forests, grasslands, marine and coastal environments, as well as a reduction of freshwater supplies and damage to coastal structures. The study notes that while humankind is very adaptable given enough time, effort, and money, "the unmanaged systems of plants and animals that occupy much of our landscape and oceans" may not be able to adapt fast enough, "making their future questionable."[39]

With respect to military threats to our national security, we routinely plan for worst-case scenarios. In the past, for example, we planned for a "bolt out of the blue" strike by the Soviets that would have theoretically destroyed half our nuclear arsenal. Prudence dictates that when dealing with major environmental problems, we also consider worst-case scenarios. As the National Academy of Sciences cautions: "The behavior of complex and poorly understood systems can easily surprise even the most careful observer." The hole in the ozone layer is one example of an unexpected outcome, and ozone depletion continues to exceed worst-case fears. In April 1991, the Environmental Protection Agency (EPA) announced that the ozone layer over U.S. latitudes is disappearing at a rate of 4 to 5 percent a year, twice as fast as had been predicted, which may result in an additional 200,000 deaths from skin cancer over the next 50 years in this country alone. Early in 1992, NASA scientists announced that they had detected record levels of ozone-destroying chemicals above the Northern Hemisphere, raising the possibility that an ozone hole could develop over populated parts of the United States sometime in the next few years.[40]

In a worst-case analysis of the greenhouse effect, the temperature would increase 5° C over the next 100 years, causing a drastic shock to the ecosystem: the earth's average temperature has changed only 5° C in 10,000 years, from the end of the last Ice Age. The academy cannot preclude the occurrence of "radical changes" to the ecosystem, such as significant melting of the Antarctic Ice Sheet "resulting in a sea level several meters higher than it is today"; "radically changed major ocean currents leading to altered weather patterns"; or a runaway greenhouse effect if initial warming melts the high-latitude tundra causing a sudden release of methane.[41] Such radical changes would lead to an ecological catastrophe of unimaginable proportions, with widespread drought, desertification, starvation, flooding, and tens of millions of environmental refugees. The academy concluded its study with the warning that "if climate change occurs, and no mitigation or adaptation actions are undertaken, a substantial reduction in real income is likely over time." This certainly could be seen as a long-term threat to U.S. economic security, especially since the academy estimates that adaptation efforts could cost the United States between $300 billion and $400 billion in the next century.[42]

Although the United States has not committed itself to controlling carbon dioxide emissions, its major industrial trading partners have. Japan has pledged to stabilize carbon dioxide at 1990 levels by the year 2000; Australia, New Zealand, and most European nations believe they can reduce their emissions by 20 percent without hurting economic growth. Germany has promised a 25-percent reduction from 1987 levels by the year 2005.[43] All of these countries produce far less carbon dioxide per capita than the United States.

Before we examine how environmental issues may have an impact on more traditional security concerns, we should also look at the problem of deforestation, the "most serious form of renewable resource decline."[44] Each year, an area the size of Austria is deforested. Deforestation exacerbates global warming by destroying plants that otherwise would have removed carbon dioxide from the atmosphere. When plants are burned or cut and allowed to decay, carbon dioxide is released into the atmosphere. Furthermore, many of the ecosystems under assault, such as the tropical rain forests, are fragile, and once destroyed may not be recoverable. They harbor an unbelievable biological diversity of species, perhaps the majority of species on the planet. Researchers found on a single tree in Peru as many ant species as are found in all of the British Isles. In ten selected one-hectare plots in Indonesia it is possible to find 700 tree species, equal to the number of tree species native to all of North America. These forests contain medicines and foods as yet unknown to us. Globally, nearly a quarter of all medical prescriptions are for compounds derived from plants and microorganisms. A very promising anticancer drug, taxol, was found in the rapidly vanishing ancient forests of the Pacific Northwest. Who knows what cures could be found in the near limitless abundance of the rain forests? There are at least 75,000 plant species with edible parts, although in the course of history humans have used no more than 10 percent of them. Today we rely heavily on a mere twenty species. Yet at the rate the rain forests are being cut down, we are losing some 4,000 to 6,000 species a year. This rate of species destruction is 1,000 to 10,000 times greater than the pre-human background rate. By the year 2000, we may have lost as many as 20 percent of all the plant species now living.[45]

Resource and Environmental Threats to National Security as It is Traditionally Defined

Wars over resources date to ancient times; the Trojan War, for example, may have been fought in part over tin.[46] The United States has not only been blessed with abundant resources but with diverse suppliers for many strategic resources. This, coupled with the inherent substitutability of one resource for another in many instances, has led a number of analysts to conclude that oil is essentially the only commodity whose cut-off (or threatened cut-off) could have a significant effect on the national welfare and the U.S. economy.[47] (Because of the special nature of oil in U.S. foreign policy, it will be treated separately in the next section of this essay.)

Many other countries, however, face growing demand for scarce resources in circumstances that may lead to conflict or ecosystem collapse, resulting in environmental refugees. Such traumas could threaten U.S. national security if these conflicts were to occur in areas of importance to the United States, or if refugees were to flee in large numbers to this country.

The word "rival" derives from a Latin word meaning "one who uses a stream in common with another."[48] A key resource security issue is the growing scarcity of fresh water, especially in the Middle East. By the year 2000, Jordan's water needs are projected to exceed supply by 20 percent, Israel's by perhaps 30 percent. The West Bank aquifer supplies 25 to 40 percent of Israel's water.[49] Before 1967, only 3 percent of the Jordan River's basin was within Israel's borders, and one reason Israel went to war that year was that Syria and Jordan were trying to divert the flow of the river.

Turkey's Ataturk Dam on the Euphrates River will irrigate 7,000 square miles—an area the size of Israel—enabling Turkey to double its farm output and electrical production. But the downstream effect on Syria and Iraq could be significant. In 1987, for instance, Turkey allegedly suggested it might curtail the flow of water to force Syria to withdraw its support for Kurdish separatists in eastern Turkey.[50]

Twenty years ago Egypt was feeding itself. By 1986, it was importing half its food. As the country's population has exploded, the Nile Delta has becoming increasingly polluted and per capita food production has declined. The Aswan Dam cannot keep up with the energy needs of the growing population and drought periods make matters worse. It is projected that by 2025 Egypt's population will have grown from 54 million to 94 million.[51] Meanwhile, water shortages in countries along the Nile's drainage system upstream of Egypt—in Sudan, Ethiopia, Uganda, Kenya, Tanzania, Zaire, Rwanda, and Burundi—are forcing them to take more water from the river. Ethiopia controls the Blue Nile tributary that is the source of about 80 percent of Nile water entering Egypt. Ethiopia has said it can do with that water whatever it wants and may divert up to 40 percent of it. In 1980, Egyptian president Anwar Sadat warned, "If Ethiopia takes any action to block our right to the Nile waters, there will be no alternative for us but to use force."[52]

Climate change can exacerbate water scarcity problems by affecting precipitation, evaporation, flooding, drought, and agricultural demand for water. The sharing of the waters of the Colorado River by the United States and Mexico, which has been a source of tension between the two countries in the past, could again be a cause of troubles if global climate change reduces the river's flow.[53]

The problem of environmental refugees also looms on the horizon. To take just a few examples, deforestation in Nepal may have worsened the 1988 flooding in Bangladesh that led to an exodus to India. In the Western Hemisphere, the Haitian exodus to the United States in the late 1970s and early 1980s was at least partly due to environmental degradation. Peasant landholders had cut most of the Haitian forests, causing erosion so severe that half the bedrock is exposed in some areas. A 1980 report to the U.S. Agency for International Development (AID) concluded: "The general prognosis for Haiti's future is apocalyptic, with little or no indication from current trends and conditions that the country will be much more than an ecological wasteland by the year 2000." [54] Today, only 2 percent of the land is still forested. Only 11 percent of the land is now able to sustain farming, and the farmable land continues to shrink. [55]

Mexico has serious environmental problems, which may contribute to the large tide of immigrants, legal and illegal, to the United States. Because much of Mexico is dry, farmland is scarce. What little exists is at risk. Soil erosion is significant in 70 percent of the good agricultural lands. Nearly 900 square miles of farmland are lost each year to desertification. About one-tenth of irrigated lands have become highly salinized. About 400 square miles of farmlands are lost each year because water is no longer available and the soil has eroded. Yet even as cropland is lost, the population grows. The country cannot support its current population of nearly 90 million. In 1986, Mexico reverted to being a net importer of food. By the year 2000, there may be another 20 million Mexicans; by 2025, the population is expected to reach 150 million. In 1990, Mexico City, with 19 million people and 32,000 industrial polluters, exceeded maximum ozone limits four days out of five, more than twice as often as Los

Angeles. Boutiques now sell oxygen for $1.60 a minute. Nevertheless, some 2,000 newcomers move to the poisoned city every day because conditions in the countryside are so bleak.[56]

Population

Resource problems in countries like Mexico and Egypt are directly connected to population growth. So, too, are deforestation, environmental degradation, and global warming. World population is expected to grow from 5.3 billion in 1990, to 6.2 billion in the year 2000, to 8.5 billion in the year 2025. This growth rate, nearly one billion people per decade, is astonishing considering that it took 130 years for the world's population to grow from one billion to two billion. Population pressure means more land is cleared for housing and agriculture, and more energy is used. Population growth was responsible for almost two-thirds of the increase in carbon dioxide entering the atmosphere between 1950 and 1985.[57]

Most of the projected population growth will take place in the developing world. Ethiopia's population is expected to rise from 47 million to 112 million in 2025, Nigeria's from 113 million to 301 million, Bangladesh's from 116 million to 235 million, and India's from 853 to 1,446 million.[58] What will happen to topsoil, forests, the climate, and regional security under such explosive conditions?

The Environment as a National Security Issue

In 1974, Gen. Maxwell Taylor complained that the National Security Council paid almost no attention "to environmental factors of such critical importance to our security as the population explosion." [59] In a paper published three years later, Lester Brown discussed at length a variety of resource and environmental problems he saw as national security threats, including deforestation; soil erosion of croplands; "the threat of climate modification," in particular, the greenhouse effect; and food scarcity, agricultural mismanagement, and starvation. "Nonmilitary threats to a nation's security are much less clearly defined than military ones," he wrote. "They are often the result of cumulative processes that ultimately lead to the collapse of biological systems or to the depletion of a country's oil reserves. These processes in themselves are seldom given much thought until they pass a critical threshold and disaster strikes." [60]

The final report of the U.N. Group of Governmental Experts on the Relationship between Disarmament and Development stated in 1981: "There can no longer be the slightest doubt that resource scarcities and ecological stresses constitute real and imminent threats to the future well-being of all people and nations. These challenges are fundamentally nonmilitary and it is imperative that they be addressed accordingly." [61] A 1982 draft report on the environment of El Salvador prepared for AID noted that "the fundamental causes of the present conflict are as much environmental as political, stemming from problems of resource distribution in an overcrowded land." [62] El Salvador has a population density that exceeds India's.

In his 1983 essay, "Redefining Security," Richard Ullman discussed the issue of resource conflict at length. [63] A still-classified 1984 CIA study,

"Population, Resources, and Politics in the Third World," is reported to anticipate conflict because of tensions over water, extreme population pressure, immigration, and resource depletion. It predicts an increase in the number of authoritarian governments and expects conflicts to become more frequent, particularly in the Third World.[64]

An early in-depth analysis of the "links between ecological decay, environmental bankruptcy and political and military instability" was presented in the 1984 Earthscan paper *Environment and Conflict*, which argued that "environmental degradation, and conflicts over shared renewable resources, have become *an important cause* of violent conflict," that these factors have largely been "neglected" by the security community, and that as the environment continues to deteriorate in the Third World, "we can *expect such conflicts to increase*." The study argues that environmentally based strife "contributed to the fall of governments in Afghanistan, Ethiopia, Iran, Nicaragua and Poland" and to political instability in Central America, the Horn of Africa, Iran, and Afghanistan. It details environmental refugee problems, such as exists between Bangladesh and India, as well as disputes over water resources in the Middle East and elsewhere.[65]

Subsequently, a significant number of studies have expanded on this theme of the growing likelihood of resource-based conflict.[66] Resource scarcity is seen as a growing threat to regional security, and by extension, to national security, since the United States has a stake in maintaining regional stability, especially in such areas of traditional national security interest as the Middle East and Central America. Many analysts recommend that the United

States take steps to assist sustainable development in the Third World, including debt relief, efforts to control population growth, and offers of U.S. ecological aid that are more comparable to that given for military aid.

Jessica Tuchman Mathews argues that security must be broadened to include not just resource and environmental issues but also "demographic issues." Population issues are a part of many of the above analyses and the primary focus of other recent analyses.[67] Population issues are considered important not only as a direct determinant of military size and power but also as a major factor in resource depletion and economic growth and, hence, political stability and domestic and interstate violence. Adherents of this viewpoint believe "development assistance and population planning" are tools of statecraft as important as new weapons systems. The fact that this line of thinking would seriously complicate the ability of the nation to assess its security policies is no deterrent to sociologist Gregory Foster, who argues that the "surest and most dangerous way to find out" how much of a threat foreign population trends pose for U.S. security "is to ignore the links that exist between population variables and security variables—even if the nature and direction of those links elude current capacity for understanding."[68]

Similarly, the security implication of global climate change has garnered the attention of analysts.[69] Some make the argument that global climate change has the potential to affect international relations and, in some cases, worsen existing conflicts or create new ones. Rising sea levels, decreased availability of fresh water, and changing agricultural patterns could increase regional rivalries and regional conflicts. In particular, global warming could create tens or even hundreds of thousands of environmental refugees, a traditional source of political instability and tension between nations.

In light of the earlier discussion of how population control efforts might limit the environmental security threat from resource depletion, it is worth noting one of the National Academy of Sciences' recommendations for addressing the greenhouse effect: "Control of population growth has the potential to make a major contribution to raising living standards and to easing environmental problems like greenhouse warming. The United States should resume full participation in international programs to slow population growth and should contribute its share to their financial and other support."[70]

The Current Debate
Over Environmental Security

Although environmental security is a relatively new study area, it is already the subject of debate. For instance, in "The Case Against Linking Environmental Degradation and National Security," Daniel Deudney, an environmental analyst, argues that "it is analytically misleading to think of environmental degradation as a national security threat, because the traditional focus of national security—interstate violence—has little in common with either environmental problems or solutions." Deudney believes that "environmental degradation is not very likely to cause interstate wars," in part because the economic decline resulting from environmental collapse might only serve to weaken a country militarily. Further, he believes "the familiar scenarios of resource war of diminishing plausibility for the foreseeable future," in part because materials have become so "substitutable," reducing dependence on any one material, and in part because "the robust character of the world trade system means that states no longer experience resource dependency as a major threat to their military security and political autonomy." Thomas Homer-Dixon from the University of Toronto replies that Deudney's perspective "ignores forms of violence other than interstate war, and he does not examine the many routes to severe conflict that do not involve the rational choice of state actors."[71]

These debates are not merely academic. From the point of view of U.S. national security interests, the Persian Gulf War does seem, at least in part, to undercut Deudney's argument that states no longer view resource dependency as a major security threat. In March 1991, a senior advisor to President Hosni Mubarek of Egypt said, "We need not only military security, but economic security. And that also means questions of the environment, and the security of water supplies. Because if water becomes scarce, it could become a source of serious conflict throughout the region." This seems to support the view of Joyce Starr, a specialist on the Middle East and water security issues, that "water security will soon rank with military security in the war rooms of defense ministries."[72] To the extent that some of Mexican emigration can be attributed to environmental and resource problems, the United States absorbs hundreds of environmental refugees every day from Mexico. Even the National Security Council appears to be open to the argument that at least some environmental concerns can be national security concerns, as evidenced by its 1989 decision to set up a committee on oceans, environment, and science.[73]

One proponent of redefining security argues that " 'environmental security' offers a more fruitful basis for cooperation and security among nations than military security because it is both a positive and inclusive concept. . . . While military security rests firmly on the competitive strength of individual countries at the direct expense of other nations, environmental security cannot be achieved unilaterally: it both requires and nurtures more stable and cooperative relations among nations."[74] Deudney believes, however, that

> the conventional national security mentality and its organizations are deeply committed to zero-sum thinking. "Our" gain is "their" loss. . . . The prevailing assumption is that everyone is a potential enemy, and that agreements mean little unless congruent with immediate interests. . . . In contrast, in the environmental sphere "we"—not "they"—are the "enemy," as Pogo reminds us. . . . If in fact resolution of the global environmental problem, and particularly the global climate change problem, requires great, even unprecedented, types of international cooperation, then nationalist sentiment and identification is a barrier to overcome. Thus, thinking of national security as an environment problem risks undercutting . . . the sense of world community that may be necessary to solve the problem.[75]

We must therefore ask: *Does the application of the phrase "national security threat" to an issue imply that the solution must necessarily involve either the traditional national security apparatus or the traditional national security approach? Or is it possible that broadening the definition of national security requires a broadening of the nation's tools and approaches devoted to solving its problems?* This is an issue relevant not just to environmental security issues but also to the issues of energy security, economic security, and the nation's drug problem.

Nor is this purely an "old way of thinking" versus a "new way of thinking" argument. The superpowers viewed the global threat posed by above-ground testing of nuclear weapons serious enough to warrant a prohibitionary treaty, and they apparently thought the threat of nuclear war from an accelerated arms race was serious enough to negotiate a treaty forcing them to severely restrict testing, production, and deployment of a variety of weapons systems, most notably antiballistic missile systems. Moreover, some would argue that renewed concern over the possibly catastrophic global ecological effects of a nuclear war, the fear of nuclear winter, was at least part of the explanation for the progress on arms reductions achieved since the mid-1980s.

To the extent that global concerns informed national security concerns in the nuclear arms race, a redefinition of security to include global warming should not inherently be an obstacle to multilateral negotiation. The Montreal Protocol on Substances that Deplete the Ozone Layer, adopted in 1987, showed both that the world could act to curtail dangerous emissions and how difficult achieving such concerted actions would be; issues related to Third World development and North-South technology transfer proved particularly hard to resolve. Given the many interests at stake ("agriculture, energy, industry, water, ecology, population, Third World development, and specific political commitments—

such as tax policy"[76]), negotiating a multilateral agreement to minimize global climate change seems certain to be far more difficult than achieving either bilateral nuclear arms reductions or the Montreal Protocol. This difficulty of achieving consensus on targets and timetables was underscored at the 1992 Earth Summit in Rio de Janeiro.

Definitional Issues

Most analysts who write on the subject do not define environmental security. Many merely catalog environmental problems and label them as security threats. To make sense of the analyses, it is useful to return to the two categories—global environmental problems, and resource and environmental threats to traditional security—with which we began.

With respect to the second category, Peter Gleick, environmental security expert at the Pacific Institute, writes: "What is required is not a redefinition of international or national security, as some have called for, but a better understanding of the nature of certain threats to security, specifically the links between environmental and resource problems and international behavior."[77] In other words, we in the United States should be more aware that resource and environmental issues can contribute to the kind of traditional security issues (conflict and instability) that we have always been concerned about. The Gulf War should serve as a further boost to that line of reasoning. If water scarcity is, as many analysts say, a threat to Middle East peace, then given the region's traditional importance to us, we should be devoting resources (foreign aid, technical assistance) to its solution.

Although the United States seems unlikely to suffer from instability because of resource scarcity, other nations are not so fortunate, and they might well want to broaden their definition of security. Such is the view of the authors of "Dimensions of National Security: The Case of Egypt." They believe that "to get a balanced picture of Egypt's security, three critical dimensions must be considered." The first two are conventional military security and political stability or governance ("the security of the government against pressures from society").

> The essential and necessary condition for the security of any state is the third dimensions of the security complex—the sustainability of the resource base in light of the pressures and "demands" of the population and the level of technology of the society. Resource security refers to the broad socioeconomic framework supporting the state, in terms of overall contextual and structural viability. The absence of this type of security will be manifested in trouble and disorder in political security due to the internal pressures and the inability of the government to contain, manage, regulate, or export pressures on the resource base. . . . In simple parlance, political security can be eroded from "above" (by threats of a military nature or transgressions on sovereignty) or from "below" (from pressures of population demands given prevailing capabilities to meet them).[78]

The issue of whether purely domestic problems should be viewed as security threats is one that crops up repeatedly in this analysis.

With respect to the first category, global environmental problems represent in general a wholly distinct security issue. It is true that for some countries, sea-level rise is a direct threat to the viability of the state, but this does not seem likely for the

United States. It is also true that in the worst-case scenario, 5° C warming and several meters' rise in sea level, Central America and the Caribbean might well produce tremendous numbers of environmental refugees who would seek entry in the United States. This would pose a traditional security threat. But this scenario is distant and unlikely.

Far more urgent is the National Academy of Sciences warning that climate change might result in a substantial reduction in real income over time. This suggests that global warming fits Richard Ullman's definition of a threat to national security, that is, "an action or sequence of events that (1) threatens drastically and over a relatively brief span of time to degrade the quality of life for the inhabitants of a state, or (2) threatens significantly to narrow the range of policy choices available to the government of a state or to private nongovernmental entities (persons, groups, corporations) within the state." If global warming turns out to be a real problem and the United States does not take early action to mitigate its effects, the policy choices available to the government to respond to it later will certainly have narrowed. Vice President Al Gore believes that environmental deterioration has become an "issue of national security" because it "threatens not only the *quality* of life but life itself."[79]

All pollution problems do not deserve to be considered environmental security threats, since that would render the term meaningless. Most pollution does not threaten a substantial reduction in real income. Nor do most environmental problems have a large extraterritorial or international component. Perhaps eliminating the phrase "over a relatively brief span of time" from Ullman's definition would provide us with more useful guidelines for determining which environmental problems could be considered serious security threats: *A threat to environmental security is whatever threatens to drastically 1) degrade the quality of life for the inhabitants of a state, or 2) narrow the range of policy choices available to the government.* Global warming and the loss of the ozone layer would certainly fit under this rubric, but most domestic pollution problems would not.

Many of the most serious threats to a nation's security—whether they be environmental or economic—are long term in nature. When a nation is faced with short-term threats, such as imminent invasion, it clearly must place those above all others. The United States is faced with very few such threats today, and so long-term threats must gain in prominence in its security policymaking.[80]

IV

Energy Security

No single issue demonstrates the interconnectedness of the new security discussions better than energy. Oil was one of the primary reasons the United States fought the Gulf War; the combustion of oil, and other fossil fuels, is the principal cause of global warming; and oil imports now account for more than half of our trade deficit. It was to a large extent the oil shock of 1973 that caused many to accept energy security and economic security as key components of national security.

One recent analyst notes that, traditionally, the "key concept in any security analysis" of energy has been "vulnerability," which "exists if there are plausible scenarios of resource trade disruptions which could be overcome only at high economic and social costs."[81] Because of the growing interconnectedness of security issues, a somewhat broader definition might be more useful. Daniel Yergin, author of the widely acclaimed book on the history of oil, *The Prize*, has suggested that "the objective of energy security is to assure adequate, reliable supplies of energy at reasonable prices and in ways that do not jeopardize major national values and objectives."[82]

Because of its tremendous domestic supply of oil, the United States did not have the kind of energy security concerns that both Germany and Japan had during World War II. In the mid-1950s, the United States still produced roughly half of all of the world's oil—twice as much oil as the Middle Eastern and North African oil states combined. By the late 1960s, the U.S. surplus production had vanished, and between 1967 and 1973, oil imports rose from 19 percent to 36 percent of total U.S. oil consumption.[83] In 1972, the chairman of the Atomic Energy Commission, James Schlesinger, urged the promotion of energy conservation for reasons of national security, foreign economic policy, and environmental improvement, but few heeded his words.[84] As late as April 1973, Charles Schultze could write, "Oil provides no exception to the basic propositions stated above, that U.S. national security interests and the rationale for the size and structure of U.S. military forces cannot be defined in terms of protecting access to markets or raw material sources abroad."[85]

One year later, after the Arab oil embargo and the rapid escalation of oil prices, Gen. Maxwell Taylor would warn, "One could hardly hope to find a better example of the seriousness of nonmilitary threats to national security than the present energy crisis."[86] Yet energy security, like many of the other elements of an expanded definition of national security, has both nonmilitary and military elements.

In 1974, Congress proclaimed that "the urgency of the Nation's energy challenge will require commitments similar to those undertaken in the Manhattan and Apollo projects."[87] In 1975, fuel efficiency standards and the strategic petroleum reserve were established. In April 1977, President Jimmy Carter uttered his now famous words: "Our decision about energy will test the character of the American people and the ability of the President and Congress to govern the Nation. This difficult effort will be the moral equivalent of war, except that we will be uniting our efforts to build and not to destroy." Carter, and his energy "czar," James Schlesinger, implemented a broad energy program aimed at reducing U.S. oil imports by eliminating price controls on U.S. domestic oil, promoting energy conservation, and supporting the development of alternative fuels, including synthetic fuels and renewable sources, such as solar energy.

But there was a strong military emphasis to Carter's energy policy as well. Within a month of the Soviet invasion of Afghanistan in December 1979, the president announced the nation's military energy policy, promulgating the Carter Doctrine: "An attempt by any outside force to gain control of the Persian Gulf region will be regarded as an assault on the vital interests of the United States of America and such an assault will be repelled by any means necessary, including military force."[88] In 1980, Carter established the Rapid Deployment Joint Task Force to make possible a quick response to any Soviet incursion. The military contribution to energy security—keeping the shipping lanes open—was laid out in the annual Defense Department report for fiscal year 1981:

> With time and a reduction in our standard of living, we could forgo or substitute for much of what we import. But any major interruption of this flow of goods and services could have the most serious near-term effects on the U.S. economy. In no respect is that more evident than in the case of oil. A large-scale disruption in the supply of foreign oil could have as damaging consequences for the United States as the loss of an important military campaign, or indeed a war. Such a disruption could be almost fatal to some of our allies. It is little wonder, in the circumstances, that *access to foreign oil*—in the Middle East, North and West Africa, the North Sea, Latin America, and Southeast Asia—*constitutes a critical condition of U.S. security.*[89]

The Carter energy policies, coupled with rising oil prices, accomplished a great deal. From 1973 to 1986, the nation's GNP grew at an average 2.5 percent a year, but U.S. energy use did not grow at all, resulting in a savings of about $150 billion per year in energy costs. By the mid-1980s, the United States was able to save the equivalent of 13 million barrels of oil a day compared with 1973 levels, making energy efficiency the largest new source of oil for the United States by far. Oil imports, which had reached 46 percent of consumption in 1977, dipped to 28 percent by 1982. Projects to boost energy efficiency funded by the Department of Energy (DOE) during the Carter years have paid off remarkably. An analysis by the Lawrence Berkeley Laboratory showed that for three projects the DOE funded in the 1970s, federal investment totaling $6 million will eventually generate savings of $82 billion—a return on taxpayer investment of 14,000 to 1.[90]

The Reagan administration largely reversed the Carter nonmilitary energy program. Efficiency standards for new cars were rolled back in the mid-1980s, federal funding for energy conservation was cut by 70 percent, and funding for solar and other renewable forms of energy was cut by 80 percent. (By contrast, Japan's funding for such research and development doubled in the 1980s; the Japanese now spend more money on solar energy than we do, as do the Germans.) These rollbacks, coupled with much-reduced oil prices in the mid-1980s, brought an end to improvements in energy use per dollar of GNP. Oil imports, which had remained at about 28 percent of overall consumption through 1985, began to rise steadily, reaching 50 percent for the first seven months of 1990 (prior to the Iraqi invasion of Kuwait), the highest level ever. America's reliance on Persian Gulf oil rose 500 percent from 1985 to 1989. In 1990, oil accounted for roughly half of our $100-billion trade deficit. The administration did continue a military energy program, guaranteeing that the United States would spend tens of billions of dollars each year safeguarding the flow of oil, ultimately reflagging eleven Kuwaiti oil tankers and providing a naval presence in the Persian Gulf for support.[91]

Saddam Hussein's invasion of Kuwait, and the subsequent economic sanctions against export of Iraqi or Kuwaiti oil, brought the issue of energy security—military and nonmilitary—to the forefront as the price of oil temporarily shot above $40 per barrel. The threat that Saddam Hussein might use the oil weapon was not the only reason the United States decided to defend Saudi Arabia and ultimately to attack Iraq, but it certainly was an important one. President Bush said during the gulf crisis: "Our jobs, our way of life, our own freedom and the freedom of friendly countries around the world would all suffer if control of the world's great oil reserves fell into the hands of Saddam Hussein" and "We cannot allow any tyrant to practice economic blackmail. Energy security is national security, and we must be prepared to act accordingly."[92]

The Current Debate
Over Energy Security

The end of the war coincided with the completion of the National Energy Strategy Review, which included eighteen meetings nationwide over a period of eighteen months in which DOE officials heard from industry, the public, and independent experts, and which resulted in 22,000 pages of testimony. The current debate over energy security has on the one side defenders of the National Energy Strategy, who essentially favor continuing the supply-side approach to energy strategy (which includes the U.S. military energy policy) and, on the other side, those who would like to see an energy security strategy that includes a strong nonmilitary component based on demand reduction.[93]

The strategy has several recommendations for expanding the use of nuclear power. It would accelerate the review process for new nuclear power plants by limiting public comment. Implementation of the strategy would also make it more difficult for states to block nuclear waste repositories within their own borders. Nuclear energy production would double from current levels by 2030; this is a 3400 percent increase over the projected decline in nuclear energy production that will occur over the next 40 years without new pronuclear policies. The use of solar power and wind power would not grow appreciably over the next 25 years.

The National Energy Strategy also has a variety of proposals for increasing domestic oil extraction, including opening for exploration part of Alaska's Arctic National Wildlife Refuge and tax credits to encourage oil recovery.[94] On the demand side, the strategy makes no proposals aimed at encouraging motorists to reduce their use of gasoline. It rejects calls for an oil import fee, higher gasoline taxes, higher fuel-efficiency standards for cars, and programs to encourage conservation and energy efficiency because "the cost would be very high—in higher prices to American consumers, lost jobs, and less competitive U.S. industries." It opposes gasoline tax increases because "significant gross national product losses were estimated to result from a large motor fuel tax increase." The bottom line is straightforward: "The National Energy Strategy review . . . revealed that our Nation and the world are likely to depend *more* on Middle East oil suppliers under any realistic scenario for the foreseeable future."[95]

The view that the United States need not take strong action to minimize dependence on imported oil is supported by some scholars. M. A. Adelman, professor emeritus of economics at M.I.T. argues that "the proportion of oil imported by the United States is of only minor importance, yet it has become the focus of debate during the present crisis. Japan and Germany import practically all of their oil, but are not perceptibly worse off economically than the United States. The world oil market, like the world ocean, is one great pool. The price is the same at every border. Who exports the oil Americans consume is irrelevant."[96] Adelman furthermore would support neither demand reduction nor supply increase strategies because "there is no shortage or gap, only a high price. . . . Subsidizing otherwise unprofitable investment, through tax breaks, for example, to replace imported oil will only aggravate the economic loss."[97]

Many analysts take a different view on the degree to which the United States should be worried about increasing reliance on Middle East oil. In 1987, James Schlesinger said:

> I believe the United States should be worried. Its role in the world is unique. Unlike Germany, Japan,

or France, all of which, incidentally, worry a great
deal about oil dependency, the United States is the
great stabilizing power in the free world. Other nations can be oil dependent. If, however, the United
States is to sustain its role in the world and to maintain the necessary freedom of action in foreign policy matters, it cannot afford to become excessively
dependent on oil imports, particularly from the
most volatile regions of the world.[98]

Schlesinger reviewed recent American history—
from the 1956 Suez crisis to the 1986 decision to
attack Libya—to illustrate his thesis. He concluded
that the solutions to our oil problem "are at hand
and are well understood." They are "to encourage
overall energy conservation, especially of oil; to promote the development and use of domestic energy
resources; and to substitute other energy resources
for imported oil."[99]

The most prominent Bush administration official to support this position is Secretary of State
James Baker. On February 5, 1991, he told the House
Foreign Relations Committee, "We should view security not just in military terms." Baker listed five
post–Gulf War challenges, four of them regional:
achieving greater regional security, arms control,
economic reconstruction, and Arab-Israeli peace.
"And a fifth and final challenge, Mr. Chairman, concerns the United States. We simply must do more
to reduce our energy dependence." Baker said a
U.S. energy strategy "should involve energy conservation and efficiency, increased development,
strengthened stockpiles and reserves, and greater
use of alternative fuels."[100]

The transportation sector accounts for nearly
two-thirds of U.S. oil use. The United States could
reduce oil consumption by two million barrels per
day by the year 2005 by raising the average fuel

economy for new cars from 27 miles per gallon to 40 miles per gallon. Such savings would amount to *more* oil than we import from the Persian Gulf and is five times the production rate possible from the Arctic National Wildlife Refuge, according to Department of Interior estimates. Moreover, the efficiency savings would be permanent, they would have a positive effective on the environment, and they would result from a straightforward extension of existing automobile technology. In contrast, the Interior Department estimated in 1991 that the Alaska National Wildlife Refuge had less than a 50 percent chance of containing economically recoverable oil.[101]

In "Make Fuel Efficiency Our Gulf Strategy," energy analysts Amory and Hunter Lovins propose establishing a system of rebates and "feebates" for cars.[102] When registering a new car, the buyer would pay a fee or receive a rebate, depending on the efficiency of the car, which would increase consumer interest in fuel-efficient cars by putting the costs of inefficiency up front. An additional rebate could be given for trading in old, fuel-inefficient cars, which would speed up the process of getting those highly polluting cars off the road.

Others believe a higher gasoline tax should be one of the aims of U.S. energy security policy. Energy analyst Daniel Yergin says, "An increase would also be an important source of revenues for an administration and Congress serious about attacking the budget deficit; each cent of additional gasoline tax translates into an additional one billion dollars in revenue." Recently, the American Assembly's noted security experts called for a $1 gas tax increase over a period of three to five years. Yergin points out that while the gas tax in the United States is about 30 cents per gallon, in Germany and Japan it is about $1.50.[103]

Many energy analysts have recommended a higher price for gasoline simply to reflect the so-called "full social cost" of gasoline, which includes the money the Defense Department spends to safeguard the oil supplies in the Persian Gulf, federal subsidies to the domestic oil industry, the health costs and environmental damage caused by petroleum combustion, and the jobs lost due to the outflow of capital from the United States to pay for imported oil.[104] This full or true cost was estimated in 1990 to be $50 to $100 per barrel *above* the actual cost. By underpricing oil, we overuse it, with negative environmental and economic consequences. Furthermore, the military spending devoted to keeping the shipping lanes open is a subsidy not merely of U.S. domestic use, but of the use of oil by our major trading competitors. Theodore Moran suggests that a U.S. gasoline tax should be called a "national security premium."[105]

The United States has a choice between enhancing energy security through devoting resources to prepare for (and if necessary engage in) military intervention in the Persian Gulf versus devoting resources to reduce its energy dependence.[106] While some believe that demand-reduction will be costly, others believe that the cost of achieving greater fuel efficiency will be *less* than the gasoline it replaces. Researchers at the University of Michigan and the American Council for an Energy-Efficient Economy have concluded that each gallon of gasoline saved by raising the average fuel efficiency of new cars from 27.5 miles per gallon to 44 miles per gallon by the year 2000 would cost 53 cents per gallon—far below the current price. Similarly, a 1991 National Academy of Sciences study on responses to global warming concluded that policies such as improving vehicle efficiency would have a cost "less than or equal to zero."[107]

The interrelatedness of energy policy and such economic security issues as the trade deficit and such environmental security issues as global warming complicates the discussion of the energy issue, which, traditionally, has focused on vulnerability to supply shocks. Oil experts predict U.S. dependence on foreign oil will reach the 60-percent mark in the late 1990s, with imports reaching perhaps 13 million barrels per day.[108] The National Energy Strategy anticipates an oil price near $30 per barrel in the year 2000. Others believe a price as high as $40 per barrel is likely by then.[109] If, in the year 2000, the price of oil is $30 per barrel and the United States is importing 9 million barrels per day, the trade deficit from oil alone will be $100 billion.

Under the National Energy Strategy, the emissions of carbon dioxide, the principal cause of global warming, are projected to rise 25 percent in the next twenty five years. Emissions reductions are achievable. Two California utilities have already pledged to reduce their carbon dioxide output by 20 percent over the next twenty years by promoting renewable power and the efficient use of energy. The Environmental Protection Agency (EPA) announced in January 1991 that by replacing the lights in one of its offices, electricity use, costs, and power plant emissions were reduced by 57 percent. The EPA said that if all businesses upgraded their lighting, about 11 percent of all the electricity used in this country would be saved and costs would drop by $18.6 billion a year; at the same time, the national output of sulfur dioxide, the principal cause of acid rain, would be cut by 7 percent, and output of carbon dioxide would fall by 5 percent.[110]

Per capita energy consumption in the United States is twice as high as that of many of our industrial competitors. If we were as efficient as the Japanese and Western Europeans, we would save nearly $200 billion a year in energy costs. As early as 1981, improvements in energy efficiency and conservation were proposed as one solution to the carbon dioxide problem.[111] Because of their relevance to a broad spectrum of issues, it is worth outlining some of the recent advances in energy technology with which we may be able to mitigate global warming.

There is a broad consensus in the technical community that the use of more energy-efficient products could save between 30 percent and 70 percent of the total electricity used in the United States at an average cost of only about two to three cents for every kilowatt hour saved (which is well under half of the cost of electricity from a new coal-fired plant). The energy efficiency of buildings could be doubled by the year 2010, saving the nation $100 billion per year and reducing carbon emissions from buildings in half.[112] Why are the savings so big? The energy loss in U.S. buildings through their windows alone equals twice the entire output of the Alaska pipeline. High-performance windows can save almost all of that energy. Compact fluorescent lightbulbs, such as those the EPA recommends, use one-quarter the energy of regular lightbulbs, and although they cost much more, they last ten times as long. It is possible, therefore, to "make money without even counting the savings in electricity."[113]

In the last ten years, the cost of wind-generated electricity has dropped roughly 80 percent, to 6 cents per kilowatt hour, below the cost of electricity from a new coal-fired plant, and is expected to fall below 5 cents per kilowatt hour by 1995. Solar thermal energy, which is generated by focusing the sun's rays onto oil-filled pipes and creating steam to drive a turbine, is down to 8 cents a kilowatt hour, which is competitive with some conventional power sources today. The cost of energy from photovoltaic cells, which convert sunlight directly to electricity, has declined from $60 per kilowatt-hour in 1970, to $1 in 1980, to 30 cents today, and will continue declining.

A variety of groups, including the National Academy of Sciences, recommend a new look at nuclear power. Since "nuclear reactor designs capable of meeting fail-safe criteria and satisfying public concerns have not been demonstrated, . . . [a] new generation of reactor design is needed."[114] Issues of cost competitiveness and waste disposal must be addressed. Were significant expansion of nuclear power to be considered as a global solution to the greenhouse effect, proliferation concerns would have to be addressed.

In April 1991, the White House included "energy technologies" in its list of twenty-two technologies that should be nurtured as "critical to the national prosperity and to the national security." Sweden is an example of how energy research and development can enhance competitiveness. It has the largest percentage of energy-efficient buildings in the world, and it exports the greatest fraction of building technology worldwide. Sweden has strict building standards, and its National Council for Building Research spends five times as much as a percentage of GNP on such research as the U.S. government and American utilities combined. While the U.S. building sector adds $6 billion to our annual trade *deficit*, Sweden's building sector, when scaled to the U.S. economy, achieves the equivalent of a $60 billion trade *surplus* annually.[115]

Definitional Issues

As traditionally defined, the energy component of U.S. security has been limited to freedom from foreign dictates. But if our national security is affected by global warming, as many analysts argue, and if it encompasses trade and competitiveness problems, then we must develop a richer definition of energy security.

As Amory Lovins noted more than a decade ago, it is energy services, rather than energy supplies that are the nation's primary interest: "People do not want electricity or oil . . . but rather comfortable rooms, light, vehicular motion, food . . . and other real things." Here then is a plausible definition for the 1990s: *The goal of energy security is to assure adequate, reliable energy services in ways that increase economic competitiveness and decrease environmental degradation.*

V

Economic Security

The question of how economic security relates to national security in the post–Cold War era has two components. The first is whether economic security concerns should now be seen as equivalent to—or even more important than—military security, an issue that is closely related to the question of whether Japan has replaced the Soviet Union as the principal threat to U.S. national security. The second is whether the United States should adopt a strategic technology or industrial policy for economic reasons (because of concerns over U.S. manufacturing competitiveness) and/or for military reasons (because the U.S. military is becoming increasingly dependent on foreign suppliers, particularly Japanese suppliers of high technology).

A Historical Perspective
on Economic Security

The term "economic security" does not seem to have been widely used in the past, perhaps in part because growth in U.S. economic power as well as economic independence were taken for granted for much of our history.[116]

The connection between America's security policies and its manufacturing policy is an old one. In January 1790, Congress instructed Alexander Hamilton to write a report on "the encouragement and promotion of such manufactures as will tend to render the United States independent of other nations for essential, particularly for military supplies." Hamilton responded with his *Report on Manufactures* of 1791, which concluded that "not only the wealth but the independence and security of a country appear to be materially connected with the prosperity of manufactures."[117]

In his farewell address, George Washington cautioned, "The great rule of conduct for us, in regard to foreign Nations, is in extending our commercial relations, to have with them as little political connections as possible."[118] This is not to say that U.S. national security and foreign policies did not have a strong military component—clearly they did—only that the importance of economic security and trade have long been present. "The concept of security has remained ill-defined even in many programs dedicated to security studies," notes Harvard history professor, Charles Maier. "Certainly, however, economic dimensions have been explicitly recognized by American leaders since at least the 1930s. They have been included by every country as a vital interest."[119] In his classic 1945 treatise, *National Power and the Structure of Foreign Trade*, the noted political economist Albert O. Hirschman argued that "foreign trade . . . may become a direct source of power." He added, "Economic warfare can take the place of bombardments, economic pressure that of saber rattling. It can indeed be shown that even if war could be eliminated, foreign trade would lead to relationships of dependence and influence between nations."[120]

Although President Harry S. Truman institutionalized the idea of containing the Soviet Union as the preeminent postwar national security goal for the United States, he believed that "national security does not consist only of an army, a navy, and an air force. It rests on a much broader base. It depends on a sound economy."[121] Historian John Lewis Gaddis points out that Washington made a "key decision to rely on the economic rather than the military instruments of containment in the late 1940s."[122] The policy of containment was based on an expansive idea of national security that could encompass the Marshall Plan and, eventually, the National Defense Education Act.

Perhaps more than any other postwar president, Dwight D. Eisenhower understood the economic dimensions of security: "Beyond a wise and reasonable level, which is always changing ... money spent on arms may be money wasted.... National security requires far more than military power. Economic and moral factors play indispensable roles. Any program that endangers our economy could defeat us."[123] Eisenhower defended his trade program by saying, "If we fail in our trade policy, we may fail in all. Our domestic employment, our standard of living, our security, and the solidarity of the free world—are all involved."[124] As one analyst of Eisenhower's defense policies wrote, "Eisenhower perceived the nation's strength and security to be based on a fine balance between its economy and its military capabilities.... The defense budget was the centerpiece of the overall Eisenhower budget and economic policy.... His feeling was that the economy was the pillar of U.S. strength and security, and unbalanced budgets threatened that pillar." [125]

The economic problems of the 1970s, especially the oil shocks, suddenly made the links between economics and security clearer to many. In April 1974, Gen. Maxwell Taylor included the "energy crisis" and "retarded economic growth, higher costs of industrial production, new deficits in international payments and increased inflation" in a list of "nonmilitary threats to national security." Two years later, Franklin P. Huddle, the director of the congressional study, *Science, Technology and American Diplomacy*, wrote: "National security requires a stable economy with assured supplies of materials for industry. In this sense, frugality and conservation of materials are essential to our national security. Security means more than safety from hostile attack; it includes the preservation of a system of civilization." In 1977, Helmut Schmidt, chancellor of the Federal Republic of Germany, argued that the events of recent years had revealed a new "economic dimension of national security" to be added to traditional elements such as the military balance: "By this, I mean the necessity to safeguard free trade access to energy supplies and to raw materials, and the need for a monetary system which will help us to reach those targets." [126]

Edwin Feulner, Jr., concluded in 1978 that "certain basic principles emerge" from an examination of case studies and current international economic issues. Among these, "the use of economic strategy as an integral part of our national security policy must be endorsed at the highest decision-making levels in the United States government and coordinated with the Congress." [127] Feulner was arguing, nevertheless, that economic strategy (including the use of U.S. foreign aid and even agricultural exports to advance foreign policy goals) should be a tool of traditional national security and foreign policies, not that national security policies should include the promotion of domestic economic strength.

In 1981, two West Point faculty members, Amos Jordan and William Taylor, Jr., noted that "broadening the concept of security to include key international economic factors, as Chancellor Schmidt has done, is now widely accepted" and that "poor economic performance in itself may cause national security problems as unfulfilled expectations or as budgetary pressures causes defense forces to shrink." Similarly, in its annual report for fiscal year 1981, the Defense Department argued that "our economic well-being and security depend on expanding world trade, freedom of the arteries of commerce at sea and in the air, and increasingly the peaceful unhindered uses of space." [128]

While the oil shocks of the 1970s refocused attention on the economic components of national security, the question of whether economic strategy should be a means of promoting traditional national security or whether promoting domestic "economic security" should be an end in itself was not settled. Indeed, many who commented on the energy problem or the issue of economic security in general were primarily talking about the military's role in sustaining economic growth (i.e., maintaining the free flow of goods worldwide), rather than a redefinition of national security *per se*. It was the remarkable events of the 1980s—the astonishing growth of the U.S. budget and trade deficits and the contemporaneous rise of Japan as a manufacturing and high-technology giant—that caused concern about the future economic power of the United States. These events raised the issue of whether Japan, with its economic weapons, was a greater threat to U.S. national security than the Soviet Union, a nation that was by then teetering on the edge of economic collapse.

The U.S. Economy in the 1980s and Beyond

What constitutes "economic security"? Almost everyone can agree that it has to something to do with a nation's prosperity and nonmilitary influence. But then what? For our purposes, we can begin with the definition of competitiveness put forth by the President's Commission on Industrial Competitiveness in 1985: "the degree to which a nation, under free and fair market conditions, produces goods and services that meet the test of international markets while simultaneously expanding the real incomes of its citizens." [129] This idea also underpins the concept of economic security.

Education, research and development (R&D), and infrastructure act synergistically to determine a nation's international competitive success; these factors are crucial for creating an environment that nurtures industries with sustainably high wages. [130] Yet the recent U.S. record in these areas is weak. The government provided a declining share of its R&D dollars to civilian technology in the 1980s, and spending on new infrastructure fell from 2.3 percent of GNP in 1963 to only 1 percent in 1989. [131] In the 1980s, American high school students consistently ranked near the bottom of the major industrialized countries of the world in their knowledge of biology, chemistry, physics, and mathematics. Korean thirteen-year-olds succeeded twice as often as their American counterparts at solving two-step math problems, such as averaging. Three times as many of the Koreans could design a simple scientific experiment. The 1983 report of the Commission on Excellence in Education, *A Nation at Risk*, said, "If an unfriendly power had attempted to impose on America the mediocre educational performance that exists today, we might have viewed it as an act of war." While it is widely believed that the United States invests more in educating its children than other nations, this is only true if post-secondary education is included. Overall, the United States ranks fifth in public and private spending per student on schooling from kindergarten through twelfth grade among sixteen industrialized nations and is tied for twelfth in spending as a percentage of GDP.[132]

Another important factor is the budget deficit, which simultaneously acts to keep interest rates high (undermining long-term investment) and to make new spending on areas such as infrastructure and the environment difficult. The national debt, which stood at under $1 trillion in 1980, is now approaching $4 trillion, and the annual interest on that debt, now more than $200 billion, is the fastest-growing portion of the budget. With a forecasted budget deficit exceeding $300 billion for 1992, and perhaps 1993, the interest on the debt may exceed the defense budget by 1995.

The overall effect of U.S. underinvestment and the budget deficit is that we are having difficulty providing economic security for most of our people.

Since the mid-1970s, real wages for roughly two-thirds of all wage earners dropped 12 percent, to 1960s' levels. According to a 1992 report by the Federal Reserve Board, "real median pre-tax income for families was virtually unchanged between 1983 and 1989." By 1990, the median income of American families was lower than it was in 1973. The Census Bureau reports that since the late 1970s, only the richest 20 percent of Americans experienced significant real income growth after taxes (growth of more than 10 percent). One indication of how difficult it has become for most Americans to maintain their standard of living was revealed in a December 1990 Census Bureau report on household net worth (assets minus debt): while the richest 20 percent of American families became wealthier between 1984 and 1988, the remaining 80 percent suffered a decline in their net worth.[133]

Family income has not fallen as fast as wages in large part because wage earners have been working longer hours. One economist notes that for 80 percent of the labor force, *just to reach their 1973 standard of living, they must work 245 more hours, or 6-plus extra weeks a year.*[134] Many families sent a second wage earner into the work force to help make ends meet. A 1992 study of working families concluded that after adjusting for increased hours of work and work expenses, "the standard of living for the bottom 80 percent of families declined or showed no improvement" from 1979 to 1989.[135]

A fundamental threat to economic security is loss of manufacturing jobs, since these are among the nation's highest paying. The manufacturing sector lost three million jobs between 1979 and 1991.[136]

Equally dismaying, *the United States was the only major industrialized nation whose manufacturing production workers experienced a drop in hourly compensation in the last decade.* The job boom of the 1980s came from the relatively low-paying service sector, where productivity growth has been terrible. Half of the jobs created between 1979 and 1987 paid wages below the poverty level for a family of four.[137]

A 1991 study found that the United States was behind or falling behind in the areas of flexible manufacturing; design for manufacturing; design of manufacturing; integration of research, design, and manufacturing; high-speed machining; precision machining and forming; and total quality management.[138] In the area of robotics and automated equipment, the United States is no longer a factor. A Congressional Office of Technology Assessment report published in 1990 noted:

> The weaknesses in U.S. manufacturing technology must be cured if the Nation is to enjoy rising living standards together with a strong, stable position in international trade. Most of the U.S. trade deficit is in manufactured goods. . . . Manufacturing also supports most of this country's commercial research and development. . . .
> For industrial nations, technology is the key to competitive success. Nations that rely on low wages to sell their goods in the world market are, by definition, poor, whereas superior technology raises productivity and thus supports rising standards of living.[139]

In 1988, the merchandise trade deficit was roughly $130 billion, and the manufacturing trade deficit accounted for about 90 percent of the total.

Manufacturing and technology are also important components in the development of sophisticated weaponry, such as that used so successfully in the Persian Gulf War. More than twenty of the weapons systems used in the war, including the F-15, F-16, and F-18 fighters, were built with foreign transistors and microchips. Many, such as the M-1 tank, could not be manufactured without Japanese machine tools. Allied officers had to call on Japan for urgently needed battery packs used in command-and-control computers, for video display terminals used to analyze real-time data from reconnaissance planes, and for semiconductors and other key components. In all, the Bush administration made nearly thirty requests to foreign governments during the course of the war for key parts.[140] Moreover, most of the weapons used in the war were based on U.S. technology developed in the 1970s. The next generation of weapons systems are increasingly relying on advanced technologies that America does not control.

The Japanese Challenge

In industry after industry, especially in high technology, the decline in U.S. market share has been accompanied by a rise in Japanese market share. From 1984 to 1989, U.S. world market share in data processing and office automation fell from 51 percent to 32 percent, while Japan's share jumped from 14 percent to 32 percent. From 1985 to 1989, the U.S. share of the world electronics market fell from 65 percent to 51 percent; Japan's share rose from 22 percent to 31 percent. From 1980 to 1989, the U.S. share of the world semiconductor market fell from 57 percent to 35 percent; Japan's share climbed from 27 percent to 52 percent. Japan's share of the worldwide market for stepping aligners used in the manufacture of computer chips soared from under 10 percent in 1979 to more than 70 percent in 1988, while America's share plummeted from over 90 percent to 20 percent. The United States experienced similar declines in the manufacture of other semiconductor equipment.[141]

The recent decline in the U.S.–Japanese trade deficit, from $57 billion in 1987 to $41 billion in 1990, did not result from a reversal in these trends. To the contrary, during this period, the Japanese increased their trade surplus with the United States in computers, office machinery, and electrical and power-generating machinery; they did, however, more than offset this by increased purchases in American cork, breakfast cereals, meats, fish, scrap metal, tobacco, fruits and vegetables, coal, and paper. In 1990, Japan's trade surplus with the United States in just three areas—computers and telecommunications equipment, cars and trucks, and industrial equipment—totaled more than $50 billion.

The future competitive climate may well be even tougher for the United States, since the Japanese continue to outinvest us. In 1990, Japan, with half the population of the United States, outinvested us in new plants and equipment by $660 billion to our $510 billion. Between 1985 and 1991, Japan's investment in new plant and equipment totaled $4,800 per worker, compared with $2,300 per worker in the United States.[142]

The U.S. labor force is expected to increase only 1 percent a year in this decade, and we are doing nothing to increase productivity beyond its current dismal growth rate of 1 percent a year. Unless something changes, this almost guarantees that the U.S.

economy cannot grow more than 2 percent a year— the same growth rate as during the Great Depression of the 1930s. If Japan is able to maintain a 4-percent annual growth rate, its economy will surpass ours in about 20 years.[143]

Current Thinking on Economic Security

There are numerous debates taking place in the academic and policy worlds on economic matters, almost all of which began before 1989. In the post–Cold War era, the two questions that are most often framed as either national security or economic security issues are: Have economic concerns surpassed military ones as the preeminent national security problem facing the country (and related to this, has Japan replaced the Soviet Union as the principal threat to U.S. security or to its superpower status?) and, Should the United States adopt a strategic technology policy or industrial policy?

In his 1990 essay, "Rethinking National Security," Theodore Sorensen makes the case for economic security. Explicitly rejecting environmental damage and drug trafficking as national security threats, he argues for a "narrow definition of the term" to include "two basic national security goals for the new multipolar era": promoting democracy and "the preservation of this nation's economic effectiveness and independence in the global market place." He argues that if we do not solve our economic problems, we will lose our "traditional sense of flexibility in foreign affairs—the ability to mount, when needed, a Marshall Plan or Manhattan Project" and "our ability to control and protect our own destiny and daily lives—even the wages, prices, jobs, profits, home ownership and higher education opportunities of our citizens—would be threatened." Although this is a dire predicament, Sorensen explicitly rejects identifying an economic enemy: "Were our independence and way of life ever militarily threatened to that extent, we would prepare for war with the enemy. But the struggle and threat are now economic, not military; moreover, declaring war—a trade war—would represent a resounding defeat for our country, dependent as it is on an open trading system. Even to name and blame a supposed "enemy" would only handicap our effort to keep that system open." Besides endorsing an effort to reduce our budget deficit and improve our educational system, Sorensen argues that "the same kind of effort that we mounted to achieve technological superiority in the military arena" must be translated into a technology policy that turns our advantage in R&D into marketable high-technology products." [144]

Edward Luttwak, a noted strategist at the Center for Strategic and International Affairs, offers a broader and more theoretical approach to the issue in "From Geopolitics to Geo-Economics." Luttwak's starting point is that "the waning of the Cold War is steadily reducing the importance of military power in world affairs." He believes that "everyone, it appears, now agrees that the methods of commerce are displacing military methods with disposable capital in lieu of firepower, civilian innovation in lieu of military-technical advancement, and market penetration in lieu of garrisons and bases." Luttwak's central question is whether the economic competition will be "World Business" ("perfect competition" or "free interaction of commerce governed only by its own nonterritorial logic") . . . "wherein any two sides can both gain (or lose) market shares concurrently," or will it instead have "the logic of conflict," which is zero-sum, "since the gain of one side is the loss of the other, and vice versa."

Luttwak essentially believes in the zero-sum outcome. States do not "regulate economic activities to achieve disinterestedly transnational purposes" but instead "seek to maximize outcomes within their own boundaries, even if this means that the outcomes are suboptimal elsewhere." States and blocs of states do not "promote technological innovation for its own sake" but rather seek "to maximize benefits within their own boundaries." He argues that "economic regulation is as much a tool of statecraft as military defenses ever were." His conclusion is that World Politics is not about to give way to World Business. "Instead, what is going to happen—and what we are already witnessing—is a much less complete transformation of state action represented by the emergence of 'Geo-economics.' This neologism is the best term I can think of to describe the admixture of the logic of conflict with the methods of commerce—or, as Clausewitz would have written, the logic of war in the grammar of commerce."

Luttwak writes that "the goal of geo-economics (aggrandizement of the state aside) could only be to provide the best possible employment for the largest proportion of the population." (Put another way, the goal of geo-economics is to promote national competitiveness, as defined earlier.) Under geo-economics, "no sphere of state action is immune: fiscal policy can be profitably used so as to place imports at a disadvantage; regulations, benefits, services, and infrastructures can all be configured to favor domestic interests in various ways; and, of course, the provision of state funds for domestic technological development is inherently discriminatory against unassisted foreign competitors." Clearly there is a difficult distinction to be drawn between state actions that are in common practice (such as R&D funding) and more aggressive "geo-economic" actions. Luttwak does not draw the distinction, but he does offer a likely set of geo-economic policies (which might be called "industrial policy," although he does not do so): "the competitive development of commercially important new technologies, the predatory financing of their sales during their embryonic stage, and the manipulation of the standards that condition their use—the geo-economic equivalents of the offensive campaigns of war."[145]

Joseph Nye, Jr., in *Bound to Lead*, published in 1990, also argues for a broader definition of security: "National security has become more complicated as threats have shifted from military ones (that is, threats against territorial integrity) to economic and ecological ones." Nevertheless, he rejects the notions of geo-economic competition and of Japan as the economic enemy: "While many Americans believe that Japan's economic strength is a greater challenge than Soviet military power, economic competition is not a zero-sum game where one country's gain is the competitor's loss." Nye's book is to a large extent an "antideclinist" response to Paul Kennedy's bestseller, *The Rise and Fall of the Great Powers*, in which the author asserted that the United States was suffering from strategic overstretch, that too many military commitments are undermining the U.S. economy. In Nye's formulation, the United States is clearly still the world's hegemon and "leadership means pointing out that the U.S. economy can afford both domestic and international security if Americans are willing to pay for them." [146]

The declinist debate has been noticeably affected by the end of the Cold War. The collapse of the Soviet Union and the Soviet empire (as well as U.S. success in the Gulf War) supports the position of those who see the United States as the primary superpower for the near future. But the principal result of those events has been to raise the importance of economic issues and to underscore U.S. weaknesses. As C. Fred Bergsten, former assistant secretary of the treasury, notes:

> America may soon be the only military superpower. Such status, however, will be of decreased utility as global military tensions are substantially reduced and international competition becomes largely economic.
>
> Moreover, the United States is in relative economic decline, caught in a scissors movement between increasing dependence on external economic forces and a shrinking capacity to influence those forces. . . .
>
> In the short to medium term, America's international economic position is likely to decline further. [147]

Bergsten's primary concern is the same as Luttwak's: "A central question for the world of the 1990s and beyond is whether the new international framework will produce conflict over economic issues or a healthy combination of competition and cooperation. History suggests that there is considerable risk of conflict, which may even spill over from the economic sphere to create or intensify political rivalries." He quotes Japanese politician Ishihara Shintaro's prediction that "the 21st century will be a century of economic warfare" and points out that "trade 'hawks' have argued, with some success, that the reduction in the security imperative now opens the way for unilateral actions to promote U.S. trade interests." Noting the possibility that the world could divide into three trading blocs, centered around the United States, Japan, and a united Europe, he quotes historian Robert Gilpin that "almost all [students of international relations] agree that a tripolar system is the most unstable configuration."[148]

To avoid this economic conflict, Bergsten proposes the development of a new international monetary arrangement and more liberal global trade (elimination of all tariffs on industrial trade, a ban on quantitative trade barriers) policed by a strengthened General Agreement on Tariffs and Trade (GATT). Domestically, Bergsten seems to be on the side of those favoring an industrial policy:

> The United States will have to increase its government spending in some areas directly related to the country's international competitiveness. Examples include expenditures on education, research and development, export finance and direct help for key industries. It is eminently logical to use part of the "peace dividend" that may result from lessened defense outlays to finance these expenditures, since they will be aimed at achieving many of the same national goals—preserving America's world role and national security—as the programs that will be cut.[149]

The analyst who may have been most influenced by the end of the Cold War is the Harvard political scientist Samuel Huntington. At the end of 1988, he wrote an article taking exception to the viewpoints of the declinists, arguing that "American hegemony looks quite secure":

> Currently, the popular choice—and the choice of the
> declinists—for the country that will supersede the
> United States is, of course, Japan. "The American
> Century is over," a former U.S. official has said. "The
> big development in the latter part of the century is
> the emergence of Japan as a major superpower."
> With all due respect to Clyde Prestowitz, this propo-
> sition will not hold up. Japan has neither the size,
> natural resources, military strength, diplomatic af-
> filiates nor, most important, the ideological appeal
> to be a twentieth-century superpower. . . .
>
> Mr. Prestowitz's prediction as to which century
> belongs to which country is likely to be less accurate
> than that of Seizaburo Sato: "The twentieth century
> was the American century. The twenty-first century
> will be the American century."[150]

Two years later, Huntington recast his position:

> The issue for the United States is whether it can
> meet the economic challenge from Japan as suc-
> cessfully as it did the political and military chal-
> lenges from the Soviet Union. If it cannot, at some
> future time the United States could find itself in a
> position relative to Japan that is comparable to the
> position the Soviet Union is now in relative to the
> United States. Having lost its economic supremacy,
> the United States would no longer be the world's
> only superpower and would be simply a major
> power like all others.[151]

Huntington's later essay is perhaps the most
detailed analysis yet to appear in support of the view
that Japan is an economic security threat. To Huntington, the primary systemic change in international affairs is "the seeming shift in the relevance
and usefulness of different power resources, with
military power declining and economic power increasing in importance." Now that the Soviet Union
is "abandoning the military competition," the
United States is rightly "obsessed with Japan for the
same reasons that it was once obsessed with the
Soviet Union. It sees that country as a major threat
to its primacy in a crucial arena of power." He con-

tinues, "In the 1950s and 1960s the American public was concerned with 'bomber gaps' and 'missile gaps' with the Soviet Union. It is now, with much greater justification, concerned with economic performance gaps with Japan." He cites a 1989 poll in which 73 percent of Americans said that "the greatest threat to American security is the economic challenge posed by Japan" and that they supported shifting resources from military purposes "to domestic investment to make America more economically competitive." [152]

Huntington warns that "an economic cold war is developing between the United States and Japan, and Americans have good reason to be concerned about the consequences of doing poorly in that competition." He cites three problems:

> First, and most specifically, American national security, in the narrow sense, could be affected if the Japanese expand their lead in a variety of militarily important technologies. . . . American national security is obviously weakened to the extent to which the United States becomes dependent upon Japanese technology for its sophisticated weapons.
>
> Second, the growth of Japanese economic power threatens American economic well-being. . . . Japanese purchase of American companies increases Japanese access to American technology and the shift of high value-added manufacturing from the United States to Japan.
>
> Third, the increase in Japanese economic power means an increase in Japanese influence and a relative decline in American influence.[153]

The third problem is the question of hegemony, and any analysis of this subject is complicated by other factors, such as military strength, which, as the Gulf War made clear, is still an important element of global influence. Hegemony is essentially the international component of the economic security question. If Huntington is correct that Japanese ascendancy is a threat to U.S. hegemony and U.S. strategic interests, then this constitutes a threat to U.S. security, traditionally defined. Huntington proposes providing "constraints on Japanese power in East Asia by continuing the US-Japanese military alliance, encouraging movement towards Korean unification, retaining a reduced military presence in East Asia, and providing an alternative source of economic and technical assistance to developing South-east Asian countries." In a sense this is a containment strategy for Japan.[154]

Huntington's second problem is the competitiveness question, and it is strictly an economic issue, which many nonstrategists have commented on. As Michael Porter of the Harvard Business School sees it, "The United States has entered a period during which its future economic prosperity may well be set for decades. . . . That America will remain a great power is not in doubt. . . . The issue instead is whether the American economy has the dynamism to maintain or raise the American standard of living, or whether the nation will slowly lose ground in relative terms."[155] The competitiveness problem is directly linked to Huntington's first problem, the military's dependence on imported parts, since both stem in part from America's loss of key high-technology manufacturing industries. The threat to American well-being is a broad threat and, for many analysts, requires a broad response. For Huntington, "The promotion of US strategic interests will involve not only foreign and defense policy but also domestic policy on the budget, taxes, subsidies, industrial policy, science and technology, child care, education, and other topics."[156]

Seymour Deitchman, retired Pentagon analyst, does not identify Japan as the economic enemy, but he takes a broad view of the U.S. security problem and its solution: "The greatest threat to our security at present is the significant decline of our economy in relation to the key ascending economies of the world." Deitchman presents one of the few analyses with specific overall cost estimates for a "revised national security posture." He labels each of the following areas as an "element of national security strategy": revitalizing the economy (domestic investment in plant and equipment); rebuilding and maintaining infrastructure (including the highway system, air-traffic and airport systems, water and sewage systems; freeing the United States from dependence on Middle Eastern oil; reduction of acid rain; toxic waste disposal; nuclear waste disposal); improving human resources (education, health care, other social welfare programs); and revising the U.S. military force structure.[157]

Industrial Policy and National Security

Many analysts see the problem of U.S. manufacturing decline in key high-technology areas, and the related problem of dependence on foreign parts for military equipment, as specific threats requiring a specific response—namely, the development of a U.S. industrial policy. According to Adm. B. R. Inman and Daniel Burton of the private-sector Council on Competitiveness: "The basic message is clear: national security can no longer be viewed in exclusively military terms; economic security and industrial competitiveness are also vital considerations.

Indeed, where technology is concerned, it is difficult to tell where military concerns stop and economic issues begin." One element of industrial policy is foreign policy. Inman and Burton, citing the FSX deal with Japan, ask the question, "Should American economic interests be given as much weight as traditional national security concerns in the formulation of U.S. foreign policy?" They conclude, "In the future, the traditional U.S. approach to foreign policy will have to give more serious consideration to strategic industrial issues, such as the strength of the American manufacturing base and the leverage of key technologies across industries." [158]

A 1989 Defense Science Board report, "Defense Industrial Cooperation with Pacific Rim Nations," concluded that "national security can no longer be viewed only in military terms, but must include economic well-being as a key component. Therefore, we must explicitly link cooperative defense technology-sharing issues with economic issues, including trade balance and market." [159]

A related element of industrial policy is export policy. In his essay, "The United States and Japan: High Tech Is Foreign Policy," former defense secretary Harold Brown argues that "technology transfer policy in the future will have to consider several factors. The impact on future U.S. economic and technological health of prohibiting U.S. exports of a broad range of medium technologies (while those same technologies are available and transferable from many other countries) should be examined." [160] In "Security: Military or Economic?" business writer Robert Kuttner asserts that in the 1970s and 1980s:

one set of Pentagon officials repeatedly gave away America's most advanced technologies to military allies as part of the plan to yoke them to a common allied defense—even though those allies were also commercial rivals. At the same moment, another set of Pentagon officials worried that certain American industries on which they depended for vital procurements were no longer viable, and they sponsored industrial policies to save them. Simultaneously, still another set of Pentagon officials tightened controls on the exports of certain high-technology products, which made it hard for the firms that produced them, on which the Pentagon depended, to stay in business.[161]

Many other analysts make similar arguments.[162] Kuttner concludes that "just as the eclipse of a Soviet military threat demands a radical redefinition of American military security, it calls for a clarification of our conception of economic security and an honest acknowledgment of the government's role in the private, peacetime economy."[163]

Yet another element of industrial policy is domestic economic policy. As Harold Brown writes:

Assuring competitiveness with Japan in semiconductors will require billions of dollars, through some combination of government and industry action. In effect this is a fine example of high-technology industrial policy aimed at the development and manufacture of technology. Some sort of guaranteed government purchases of products at a price and over a time frame that assures corporate investment in new generation of chips and in the necessary capital equipment may be required, as will selective waivers of antitrust barriers.[164]

Of course, there are many others who see industrial policy as anathema and the "national security" justification as a convenient excuse. As Nye complains, "Every industry is likely to plead special circumstances, and national security too easily becomes the first refuge of protectionist scoundrels." [165]

The key question raised by supporters of industrial policy is, are there some technologies that are central to U.S. national security—both as it is traditionally defined and as it is more broadly defined to include economic security? A 1989 report by the National Advisory Committee on Semiconductors, "A Strategic Industry at Risk," began with the statement:

> The semiconductor industry is strategic to America. The industry is the foundation of the information age, playing a crucial role in the consumer electronics industry, and other industries that have a high electronic content in their products. America's national security also depends on the semiconductor industry. United States and NATO forces rely on the technological advantage of advanced semiconductors to offset the numerical superiority of potential adversaries. [166]

In *The Japan That Can **Really** Say No*, the Japanese politician and author Ishihara Shintaro wrote of the Persian Gulf War: "What made [the Americans'] pinpoint bombing so effective was PTV, a high-quality semiconductor used in the brain part of the computers that control most modern weapons. There were 93 foreign-made semiconductors in the weapons used by the United States. Among them, 92 were made in Japan." America "should wake up from this illusion" of superpower status because it "had to ask other countries to contribute money so it could fight, and it depended on foreign technology to carry out its war strategy." Concern about growing U.S. dependence on Japanese components inspired political analyst David Gergen, in "America as a Techno-Colony," to conclude that "now we need a national economic strategy for survival. America must never again be a colony."[167]

Theodore Moran writes that "one challenge to U.S. national security on the international economic agenda is the globalization of the defense industrial base." Yet he expresses a concern shared by many analysts: "There is no evidence the U.S. government can pick 'winners' for public support appropriately, or ensure that political forces do not divert such support to 'losers' instead." He proposes an analytically based middle ground:

> In all cases of external interference, the threat from foreign dependence is genuine only when there is a concentration within a very few nations of external suppliers of technology, products or inputs. When sources of supply have been well dispersed internationally there has been no ability to control, to delay or to deny, and hence no real peacetime threat. As a rule of thumb, when there are more than four foreign companies or four foreign nations supplying more than fifty percent of the world market, they will lack the ability to collude effectively even if they wish to exploit or manipulate recipients. This "four-fifty" rule provides a useful guide for designing U.S. policies.
>
> For American industries that are being "wiped out" by imports, those in which the sources of external supply are concentrated do represent a source of concern and should be eligible for legitimate "national security protection. . . . By this concentration test, semiconductor equipment manufactures would qualify for national security protection, textiles and footwear manufactures would not.

Moran believes that whenever "national security trade protection" is granted, a tariff, rather than a quota, should be imposed since tariffs are less distorting and the "rents go to the home government instead of to the foreign firms."[168]

A consensus does seem to be developing that the United States needs a coherent economic strategy aimed at increasing high-wage jobs. Recently, two business magazines, *Business Week* and *Forbes*, published articles endorsing a U.S. industrial policy.[169] And in April 1991, the White House, long an opponent of industrial policy, released a list of more than twenty areas of technological development that should be supported as "critical to the national prosperity and to national security." In a letter accompanying the list, William Phillips, chairman of the National Critical Technologies Panel, states: "We most recently have been reminded, by the spectacular performance of U.S. coalition forces in the Persian Gulf, of the crucial role that technology plays in military competitiveness. It is equally clear that technology plays a similar role in the economic competitiveness among nations."[170] It therefore appears that the United States will be adopting at least the initial stages of an industrial policy for national security reasons (although the White House's language—by distinguishing prosperity from security—suggests no acceptance of the idea of broadening the definition of national security).

Japan and Comprehensive Security

Given the growing salience of the competition from Japan, a brief comment on the Japanese view of national security seems worthwhile. Some analysts accuse the Japanese of systematically employing unfair trading practices, while others dispute those accusations.[171] A number of observers link Japan's trade policy with its security policy. The *Economist* notes "that the country's security depends on its economic strength is the main premise of Japanese foreign policy." According to Harold Brown, "Japan continues to be motivated largely by the conviction that so long as it is able to lead in the competition for export of manufactures its security can be preserved." And Selig Harrison and Clyde Prestowitz argue that "increasingly in recent years, Japan has sought to redefine the meaning of security in economic and political rather than in military terms. 'Comprehensive security' is the new watchword." [172]

Japan's comprehensive security doctrine, which emerged in the late 1970s, consists of both military and economic security policies. Its nonmilitary goals include attaining energy security and food security. As one analysis of the doctrine concludes:

> Comprehensive national security for Japanese decision makers, therefore, appears to include not only overt threats from an increasingly menacing Soviet military machine or from major geophysical catastrophes, but also to include major threats to the economic livelihood and standard of living of the Japanese people from the denial of access to markets for Japanese goods. . . . It implies, too, that it will be necessary to take positive steps to shape a significant part of the national environment in such a way as to protect national interests from international competition, not only in one's own market or within one's own territory, but also in other markets and in other territories. [173]

The Japanese have debated whether to institute a "comprehensive security cost" of roughly 3 percent of GNP, which would include "expenditures for 'economic security' items (e.g., food and resource stockpiling, energy research, etc.), Official Development Assistance (ODA), and military defense." [174]

Definitional Issues

There are two economic aspects of national security—competitiveness and economic independence. Competitiveness, defined as "the degree to which a nation produces goods and services that meet the test of international markets while simultaneously expanding the real incomes of its citizens" fits into the broader or nontraditional concept of national security, since it has to do with a nation's domestic prosperity and, as such, it might well be identified with economic security.[175]

A comprehensive definition of economic security must include two other elements: sustainability and equity. Economic security will not long endure if it is achieved in an environmentally unsustainable fashion, such as by using up nonrenewable resources or by destroying our ecosystem. And economic security cannot be achieved by ignoring our poorest citizens.[176] America's recent record in this area is unacceptable: the poorest 20 percent of Americans have become poorer since the 1970s, income inequality has grown steadily in the 1980s, one in five children lives in poverty, and U.S. income distribution is among the worst of the industrialized nations.[177] Taking all these things into consideration, a comprehensive definition of economic security might be: *Economic security measures a nation's ability to improve the living standards of its citizens in an equitable and sustainable fashion.*

The other economic aspect of national security, economic independence, was defined by Sorensen as "the flexibility to make decisions and to fend for oneself." It represents our ability to influence world events favorably, and this in some sense fits into the traditional definition of security. As Harold Lass-well wrote in 1950, "The distinctive meaning of national security is *freedom from foreign dictation.*" [178]

The economic threats to U.S. national security are interconnected and severe. Although I have separated the two components, competitiveness and independence, it is unlikely that we could achieve one for very long without the other. The erosion of U.S. manufacturing is degrading the quality of life of Americans because high-value-added manufacturing jobs are essential for sustaining high real incomes. Our policy choices narrow as the United States declines economically relative to other countries, and we lose our power to influence world events. The erosion of the U.S. semiconductor and high-technology manufacturing base not only threatens our economic security, it also affects our capacity to make and use sophisticated weaponry.

The economic component of national security might therefore be defined as the ability to provide a rising standard of living for the population as a whole while maintaining independence from foreign economic coercion. This construction leads us to a modified version of Richard Ullman's definition of national security: the ability to maintain or expand (1) the quality of life of the inhabitants of a state, and (2) the range of policy choices available to the government. [179]

This definition of national security encompasses both military and nonmilitary threats, including short-term military threats, such as the threat of conventional or nuclear attack and long-term political/military threats, such as containing the Soviet Union. [180] It also covers traditional energy security concerns: the fear that if foreign oil were cut off, price rises and shortages would reduce the U.S.

standard of living, at least in the short run, or the fear that the mere threat of an oil cut-off could give other nations leverage over the United States, limiting our options in a crisis. And it encompasses the threat posed by global warming—to reduce living standards and to constrict our ability to act independently.

VI

A New National Security Agenda

Historically, labeling a problem a "national security threat" has implied that it takes precedence over other problems and, therefore, that dealing with it may entail more than normal attention and sacrifice by the nation. Winning the Cold War was identified as America's principal postwar national security task and, as Secretary of State Dean Acheson said in 1947, maintaining a "counterbalance to the communistic power" would take "money, imagination, American skill and American technical help and many, many years."[181] Today we are again faced with the challenge of determining which of the problems confronting us are genuine "national security threats" so as to decide which problems necessitate this level of national effort.

It is, of course, possible to discuss the major problems we face *without* labeling them national security threats. This would absolve us of the difficult task of updating the definition of national security. But if there exist serious threats to the well-being of most Americans, these are threats to our nation's security by anyone's definition. To say that the only valid national security threats are military ones is to give national security a definition it has not had for at least two decades and perhaps not for two hundred years.

At the same time, it is important to rescue the term "national security" from overuse. As George

Orwell pointed out in his classic 1946 essay, "Politics and the English Language,"

> in our time, political speech and writing are largely the defence of the indefensible. Things like the continuance of British rule in India, the Russian purges and deportations, the dropping of the atom bombs on Japan, can indeed be defended, but only by arguments which are too brutal for most people to face, and which do not square with the professed aims of political parties. Thus political language has to consist largely of euphemism, question-begging and sheer cloudy vagueness.... Political language—and with variations this is true of all political parties, from Conservative to Anarchist—is designed to make lies sound truthful and murder respectable, and to give an appearance of solidity to pure wind.[182]

These lines apply well to many post-1945 uses of the phrase "national security." It may be too late to save "national security" from becoming meaningless. Indeed, it may be 45 years too late. Ever since it came into widespread usage in the late 1940s, the term has been employed indiscriminately by our political leaders to justify whatever policies they wished to pursue. Therefore, if the current debate is to result in a sensible national political agenda, the phrase—and its recent derivatives, "environmental security," "energy security," and "economic security"—should be carefully defined by its users.

And first we must decide whether we are talking about a partial or a total redefinition. Even if we are only aiming at the former, America's competitiveness problem must be addressed because it leads to a degradation of the nation's defense-related industrial base and thus undermines our political independence (in the same way that dependence on foreign oil does). In other words, we may still think of security in its traditional sense of military security and freedom from foreign dictates, but we must also require a better understanding of certain economic threats to that security. If, on the other hand, we are aiming at a total redefinition, the competitiveness problem takes on an added dimension because in a larger sense it undermines the quality of life of many—if not all—of our citizens. In this context, the idea of national security is expanded to include economic security, with the implication that economic revitalization must be an end in itself, as opposed to being merely the underpinning of traditional security concerns.

Similarly, we can limit our discussion of environmental issues—as they relate to national security—to achieving a better understanding of the nature of certain threats to security, specifically the links between environmental and resource problems and regional security. But if we expand the idea of national security to include environmental security in its own right, then global warming becomes a threat to security that is to be avoided as much as, say, nuclear war. In other words, environmental sustainability also becomes an end in itself, more than simply a means of promoting traditional security and regional stability.

The difference between the two approaches is fundamental. The partial redefinition of national security is really more of an expansion of the traditional definition than a true redefinition. Under this approach, we may see the wisdom of supporting certain industries that are key to building sophisticated weaponry and of promoting wise resource use (and population control) around the world, but only as a means of promoting military strength and political stability.

Under the second approach, economic security (i.e., competitiveness) and environmental security (i.e., sustainability) become as important as military security and political independence. Indeed, to the extent that the demise of the Warsaw Pact significantly reduces any short-to-medium term concerns about U.S. military security and political independence, economic and environmental security concerns might well be seen as being of paramount importance to the United States. As former Soviet foreign minister Eduard Schevardnaze pointed out in 1988,

> the struggle between two opposing systems is no longer a determining tendency of the present day era. At the modern stage, the ability to build up material wealth at an accelerated rate on the basis of front-ranking science and high-level techniques and technology, and to distribute it fairly, and through joint efforts to restore and protect the resources necessary for mankind's survival acquires decisive importance.[183]

The debate over what constitutes a national security problem in the post–Cold War era is not a purely semantic or academic matter, for two reasons. First, the debate will help determine which problems facing this nation in the next decade and into the next century will have access to "money, imagination, American skill." This is a particularly important issue in an era of huge budget deficits, when funding national priorities has become at best a zero-sum game. Second, the debate will help determine the approach we as a nation will adopt to solve our domestic problems. This is best seen in the case of industrial policy and energy policy. The federal government heavily supports nuclear power but not solar energy; it promotes aerospace industry but not advanced manufacturing. Many policymakers deny that we have an industrial policy perhaps because they do not use that label for policies designed to achieve national security goals, such as the development of traditional energy supplies or superior military technology. This is another reason why a redefinition of security is required: to spur us to change our industrial policy.

In conclusion, I wish to enumerate a number of questions that must be addressed by "experts" and laymen alike if we are to reach a new consensus on what constitutes a national security threat.

What is an Adequate Definition of National Security in the Post–Cold War Era?

Here are two possibilities:

- A threat to national security is whatever threatens to significantly (1) degrade the quality of life of the people, or (2) narrow the range of policy choices available to their government.

- The objective of national security is to sustain freedom from foreign dictation and improvement of living standards in an environmentally sustainable fashion.

What Are the Major Post–Cold War National Security Threats?

Even a sound definition of national security may remain ambiguous. Therefore, those who attempt to define the term should make clear what they consider to be *new* national security threats. I believe that the two new (and pre-eminent) post–Cold War *nonmilitary* national security threats are (a) America's declining international competitiveness and (b) global climate change. The overuse of oil also constitutes a national security threat under both traditional and new security thinking. (On the other hand, little is gained by labeling America's addiction to drugs a national security problem.)

To What Extent are Economic Growth and Environmental Sustainability Compatible?[184]

If we raise these two issues to the status of national security concerns, their interrelationship must be better understood. This is partly the domain of environmental economists, who are attempting to develop the concept of a "green" GNP that takes into account the harm that economic activity does to the environment, as well as the transitory nature of growth achieved in an unsustainable fashion, such as through natural resource depletion. To a large extent, global climate change deserves to be considered a major national security problem because, as the National Academy of Sciences warns, it threatens a substantial reduction in real income for the American people.

By almost any definition of the terms, environmental security and economic security are not just compatible but inseparable.[185] The goal of economic security is for each generation to achieve a higher quality of life than the previous one, a goal that cannot be achieved in an unsustainable fashion. Moreover, in the next century, a key component of international trade—and a major source of high-paying jobs—will be the manufacture of technologies that improve the environment, such as renewable energy. Japan is heavily investing in such technologies. In June 1991, the Ministry of International Trade and Industry (MITI) published its

"Long-term Outlook for Energy Supply and Demand," in which it emphasized reconciling the
goals of "affluence," preservation of the global environment, and energy security.[186] The United States
must now decide if it also believes that economic
security, environmental security, and energy security are compatible.

What Type of Energy Policy is Needed?

In the broadest sense, the main objective of needed
policies to achieve energy security is to assure adequate, reliable energy *services* in ways that maximize
economic competitiveness and minimize environmental degradation. The benefits of cutting oil use
and of developing new technologies for energy conservation and renewable energy production are very
high under almost any conceivable redefinition of
security. We must develop an energy program based
on a clear understanding of costs and benefits.

We must also decide what commitments the
United States should be prepared to make to minimize global warming. The remarkable advances in
energy-efficient and renewable-energy technologies
achieved over the past decade that have allowed two
California utilities to promise a 20-percent reduction in carbon dioxide emissions over the next
twenty years make a nationwide commitment to a
similar level of reductions plausible.

What Type of Industrial Policy is Needed?

Although there is widespread support for a minimal
industrial policy—increasing civilian R&D—there
is far less support for the maximum industrial policy—that is, direct federal funding and trade protec-

tion for key industries. It is incumbent upon us to spell out exactly what industrial policy the federal government should adopt, what its implications are for U.S. trade and export policies, what specific technologies (and/or industries) should be targeted, how U.S. manufacturing excellence can be restored, and how much it will all cost.

What Should America's Relationship be with Japan?

Are we adversaries, competitors, or partners? How can a trade war (i.e., the pursuit of geo-economic policies) be avoided? Does a strong domestic industrial policy increase the likelihood of a trade war (by fostering nationalism) or does it diminish it (by decreasing the economic problems that would otherwise fuel such a war)?

Nobutoshi Akao has noted that " 'economic security' is an expression used more often in Japan than in any other advanced industrialized country." [187] As a nation whose military spending was constrained, and which depends on imports for so many vital raw materials, this emphasis is not surprising. Nevertheless, Japan's doctrine of economic security or comprehensive national security deserves more attention. [188]

How Appropriate is our Current Supply-Side Approach to Drugs?

Do we need more funds, or merely a change in approach and funding priorities, so that 70 percent of the federal antidrug budget goes to reduce demand and 30 percent to reduce supply, rather than the reverse? What should our policy be with respect to the Central and South American suppliers of illicit drugs?

The apparent ineffectiveness of our interdiction efforts is suggestive. So long as we continue to define the drug problem in traditional security terms, we will continue to try to shut down drug trafficking by military means—the "supply-side" approach. But if we define the problem as domestic overuse, this would imply at the very least that we should seek a balance between funding for interdiction and funding for demand reduction. Of course, some may not consider domestic drug use a "new" national security threat, or they may see it as a symptom of the larger economic security problem of the declining standard of living of the bottom 20 percent of Americans and the loss of good-paying jobs.

How Should The Federal Government Reorganize to Meet the New Security Threats?

Many have called for a revamped National Security Council. Gen. Maxwell Taylor wrote in 1974 that "with an appropriate expansion of membership to give representation to the domestic and environmental sectors and perhaps with a modification of title (I would prefer 'National Policy Council'), the Council could be held to a more exacting compliance with its 1947 mandate." More recently, both Joseph Nye and the Council on Competitiveness have made a similar suggestion. Samuel Huntington believes that just as the United States created the National Security Council, the Defense Department, and the CIA in the 1940s to help win the Cold War, "meeting the threats to its interests in the post–Cold War era will probably require institutional innovations no less significant." [189] Many policymakers have also called for a civilian version of Defense Advanced Research Projects Agency (DARPA) to promote domestic technology policy. Any reformulation of U.S. security policy should detail what new organizations or modifications of existing organizations are required, and review the role of the U.S. intelligence community.

What Are the Budgetary Implications of Redefining Security?

It could be argued that this is the most important question of all. Everyone who writes on the subject of the U.S. economy—declinists and antideclinists alike—calls for reducing the federal budget deficit, but few have offered a prescription for how to do so. Indeed, most experts call for expanded spending in areas such as civilian R&D. And although some analysts point out that the United States is the most lightly taxed industrial nation in the world, they rarely offer tax proposals of their own.

A major point of redefining security is to redefine budgetary priorities. Moreover, while the budget deficit itself may not be a true national security problem, it certainly "significantly restricts the range of policy choices available to the government." As Seymour Deitchman (and others) have argued, military spending cuts alone cannot provide all the money necessary to revitalize this country. Any comprehensive analysis of security should explain how much money is needed to balance the budget and deal with our newly emerging security problems and what combination of spending cuts and tax increases should be undertaken to accomplish those ends. It should offer specific recommendations for defense spending levels and for spending in such areas as infrastructure, research and development, and the environment; and it should spell out whatever tax increases may be necessary.

Notes

1. It is interesting that the two U.S. foreign *military* operations of the post–Cold War era—Panama and Iraq—both had domestic *nonmilitary* origins: America's dependence on imported drugs and America's dependence on imported oil.
2. W. W. Rostow, *How It All Began: Origins of the Modern Economy* (New York: McGraw-Hill, 1975), p. 191.
3. Nicholas J. Spykman, *America's Strategy in World Politics: The United States and the Balance of Power* (New York: Harcourt, Brace, 1942). See also Albert O. Hirschman, *National Power and the Structure of Foreign Trade* (Berkeley: University of California Press, 1945, expanded edition, 1980).
4. Daniel Yergin, *Shattered Peace: The Origins of the Cold War and the National Security State* (Boston: Houghton Mifflin, 1977), p. 194, and Wade Greene, "An Idea Whose Time Is Fading," *Time*, May 28, 1990, p. 90.
5. Robert Post, "National Security and the Amended Freedom of Information Act," *Yale Law Journal*, vol. 85 (January 1976), p. 410.
6. Harold D. Lasswell, *National Security and Individual Freedom* (New York: McGraw-Hill, 1950), p. 75.
7. Arnold Wolfers, *Discord and Collaboration* (Baltimore: Johns Hopkins University Press, 1962), p. 147. (The original version of this essay dates from 1952.)
8. Barry Buzan, *People, States, and Fear: The National Security Problem in International Relations* (Chapel Hill: University of North Carolina Press, 1983), pp. 4, 9. See also Charles Schultze, "The Economic Content of National Security Policy," *Foreign Affairs*, vol. 51 (April 1973), pp. 529–30: "The concept of national security does not lend itself to neat and precise formulation.... The United States has basic national security interests which ... revolve principally around intangibles, uncertainties and probabilities

rather than around concrete threats readily foreseeable and easily grasped."

9. Post, op. cit., pp. 406, 408.

10. Walter Lippmann quoted in Morton Berkowitz and P. G. Bock, "National Security," in David L. Sills, ed., *International Encyclopedia of the Social Sciences* (New York: Mac-Millan, 1968), vol. 11, p. 40; National Security Council's "working definition," as given in Peter G. Peterson, with James Sebenius, "Rethinking America's Security: The Primacy of the Domestic Agenda," in Graham Allison and Gregory F. Treverton, eds., *Rethinking America's Security* (New York: Norton, 1992); Wolfers, op. cit., p. 150; Berkowitz and Bock, op. cit., p. 40; Amos A. Jordan and William J. Taylor, Jr., *American National Security* (Baltimore: Johns Hopkins University Press, 1981), p. 3; and Charles S. Maier, *Peace and Security Studies for the 1990s*, unpublished paper for MacArthur Fellowship Program, Social Science Research Council, June 12, 1990, p. 12. For other definitions of national security, see Buzan, op. cit., pp. 216–17.

11. Richard H. Ullman, "Redefining Security," *International Security*, vol. 8 (Summer 1983), p. 133.

12. Maxwell D. Taylor, "The Legitimate Claims of National Security," *Foreign Affairs*, vol. 52 (April 1974), pp. 592–94, and Lester Brown, *Redefining National Security*, Washington, D.C.: Worldwatch Paper 14, October 1977.

13. Jessica Tuchman Mathews, "Redefining Security," *Foreign Affairs*, vol. 68 (Spring 1989), p. 162, and Theodore H. Moran, "International Economics and National Security," *Foreign Affairs*, vol. 69 (Winter 1990/91), p. 74.

14. Lasswell, op. cit., p. 56.

15. Louis Kraar, "The Drug Trade," *Fortune*, June 20, 1988, p. 37, as cited in Scott B. MacDonald, "Slaying the Drug Hydra," *SAIS Review*, (Winter-Spring, 1989), p. 65. See also Raphael F. Perl, "United States International Drug Policy: Recent Developments and Issues," *Journal of Interamerican Studies and World Affairs*, vol. 32 (Winter 1990), p. 135.

16. Reagan's 1986 directive quoted in Waltraud Q. Morales, "The War on Drugs: A New National Security Doctrine?" *Third World Quarterly*, vol. 11 (July 1989), p. 155; Cheney quoted in Michael T. Klare, "Fighting Drugs with the Military," *The Nation*, January 1, 1990, p. 8; and Pentagon report quoted in "Excerpts from Pentagon's Plan: 'Prevent the Re-Emergence of a New Rival,'" *New York Times*,

March 8, 1992. In a February 1990 speech before the Commonwealth Club in San Francisco, President Bush said: "Now, let me tell you something about the strategy behind our 1991 defense budget. First, new threats are emerging beyond the traditional East-West antagonism of the last 45 years. These contingencies must loom larger in our defense planning. . . . Then there are narcogangsters that concern us all, already a threat to our national health and spirit. And now they are taking on the pretensions of a geopolitical force [a] whole new force to effect change, and they must be dealt with as such by our military in the air, on the land and on the seas." On the other hand, Klare quotes, among others, Secretary of Defense Frank Carlucci as having said in 1988, "That is not the function of the military. We are not the frontline agency in the war on drugs" (op. cit., p. 10). For a similar point, see Bruce M. Bagley, "The New Hundred Years War? U.S. National Security and the War on Drugs in Latin America," *Journal of Interamerican Studies and World Affairs*, vol. 30, Spring 1988.

17. Bagley, op. cit., p. 165; Perl, op. cit., p. 125; and "The Newest War," *Newsweek*, January 6, 1992, pp. 18–23.

18. MacDonald, op. cit., p. 68.

19. Juan G. Tokatlian, "National Security and Drugs: Their Impact on Colombian–U.S. Relations," *Journal of Interamerican Studies and World Affairs*, vol. 30, (Spring 1988), pp. 134, 141.

20. Perl, op. cit., p. 129. See also Bruce M. Bagley, "Dateline Drug Wars: Columbia: The Wrong Strategy," *Foreign Policy*, no. 77 (Winter 1989/90), pp. 154–71, and Michael J. Dziedzic, "The Transnational Drug Trade and Regional Security," *Survival*, vol. 31 (November/December 1989), p. 544. Ironically, the U.S. counternarcotics support may actually be *helping* the drug cartels by providing U.S. military training to Bolivian recruits who will end up working in the drug industry. According to *Newsweek*, of the 900 Bolivian soldiers now being trained by the United States, 85 percent are conscripts with one-year hitches. Many of these conscripts have relatives working in the drug trade who may hire them as security guards, "paying a premium for U.S. know-how." The article quotes one U.S. advisor: "With few exceptions, all we're doing is training the bad guys" ("The Newest War").

21. Dziedzic, op. cit., p. 544.

22. Donald Mabry, "The U.S. Military and the War on Drugs in Latin America," *Journal of Interamerican Studies and World Affairs*, vol. 30 (Summer/Fall 1988) p. 71.

23. Perl, op. cit., p. 125.

24. Moran, op. cit., pp. 88–89.

25. Turner quoted in "Cocaine Manufacturing Is No Longer Just a Colombian Monopoly," *New York Times*, June 30, 1991.

26. General Accounting Office, "The War on Drugs," GAO/NSIAD-91-233 (Washington, D.C., July 1991).

27. For instance, Frank C. Conahan, the assistant comptroller general, told Congress in October 1991, "U.S. counternarcotics programs in Peru have not been effective, and it is unlikely that they will be until Peru overcomes serious obstacles beyond U.S. control." Conahan said of counternarcotics aid to Columbia: "There is little assurance that the aid is being used effectively and as intended." See "The Drug War," statement of Frank C. Conahan before the Legislation and National Security Subcommittee, House Committee on Government Operations, October 23, 1991 (GAO/R-NSIAD-92-2). See also "Cocaine Manufacturing," *New York Times*, op.cit., and "The Newest War," *Newsweek*, January 6, 1992.

28. Testimony of Robert Gates before the Senate Armed Services Committee, January 22, 1992. After two years of intense U.S. anti-drug efforts in South America, the State Department and White House estimate that cocaine production is stuck on a high plateau of at least 700 metric tons (and may actually be rising), while U.S. consumption is 500 metric tons (European and Asian consumption make up the difference).

29. Morales, op. cit., p. 149.

30. Jessica Tuchman Mathews, "Acts of War and the Environment," *Washington Post National Weekly Edition*, April 15 21, 1991, p. 27. In the 1980s, the environmental consequences of warfare received renewed attention because of nuclear winter, the theory that a large-scale nuclear war could raise enough dust and smoke to radically alter the earth's climate.

31. A. H. Westing, ed., *Cultural Norms, War and the Environment* (Oxford: Oxford University Press, 1988), pp. 166–67. "Environmental modification technique" is defined as "any technique for changing through the deliberate manipulation of natural processes the dynamics, composition

or structure of the earth, including its biota, lithosphere, hydrosphere and atmosphere, or of outer space."

32. Cheryl Silver, with Ruth DeFries (for the National Academy of Sciences), *One Earth, One Future: Our Changing Global Environment* (Washington, D.C.: National Academy Press, 1990), p. 103.

33. Stephen Schneider, "Cooling It," *World Monitor*, July 1990, p. 32.

34. As cited in David Wirth, "Catastrophic Climate Change," in Michael T. Klare and Daniel C. Thomas, eds., *World Security* (New York: St. Martin's Press, 1991), chapter 17, p. 386.

35. The National Academy of Sciences study, *Policy Implications of Greenhouse Warming*, (Washington, D.C.: National Academy Press, 1991).

36. Christopher Flavin and Nicholas Lenssen, "Designing a Sustainable Energy System," in Lester Brown et al., *The State of the World 1991* (New York: W. W. Norton, 1991), p. 24. The Spring 1991 issue of *Climate Alert* points out that the IPCC study was also peer-reviewed by more than 200 scientists. For an alternate view, see Andrew Solow and James Broadus, "Global Warming: Quo Vadis?" *The Fletcher Forum*, Summer 1990, pp. 262–69.

37. Florentin Krause et al., *Energy Policy in the Greenhouse* (El Cerrito, Cal.: International Project for Sustainable Energy Paths, September 1989), p. I.1–15.

38. Gareth Porter, "Post Cold War Global Environment and Security," *Fletcher Forum*, Summer 1990, p. 336, and Jodi Jacobson, "Holding Back the Sea," *The Futurist*, September–October 1990, p. 23.

39. National Academy of Sciences, *Policy Implications of Global Warming*, p. 44.

40. Ibid., p. 24; "Ozone Destruction Worsens," *Science*, April 12, 1991, p. 204; and "The Vanishing Ozone," *Time* cover story, February 17, 1992, pp. 60–68.

41. National Academy of Sciences, *Policy Implications of Global Warming*, pp. 22–24.

42. Ibid., pp. 28, 98–101.

43. Lester Brown et al., *State of the World 1992* (New York: W. W. Norton, 1992), p. 180, and "The Politics of Climate," *New Scientist*, October 27, 1990, p. 21.

44. Mathews, "Redefining Security," p. 164.

45. Paul R. Ehrlich and Edward O. Wilson, "Biodiversity Studies: Science and Policy," *Science*, August 16, 1991, p. 760; Edward O. Wilson, "Threats to Biodiversity," *Sci-*

entific American, September 1989, pp. 108–16; and Mathews, "Redefining Security," p. 165.

46. Hanns Maull, "Energy and Resources: The Strategic Dimensions," *Survival*, vol. 31 (November/December, 1989), p. 500.

47. Ullman, op. cit., p. 144.

48. Jessica Tuchman Mathews, "War and Water in the Middle East," *Washington Post National Weekly Edition*, May 6–12, 1991.

49. Joyce Starr, "Water Wars," *Foreign Policy* (Winter 1991), p. 24, and Norman Myers, "Environment and Security," *Foreign Policy* (Spring 1989), p. 28.

50. Starr, op. cit., p. 31.

51. *World Resources 1990–91* (New York: World Resources Institute, in collaboration with the U.N. Environment Programme and the U.N. Development Programme, 1990), pp. 254–255.

52. Myers, op. cit., pp. 30–32.

53. Peter H. Gleick, "The Effects of Future Climatic Changes on International Water Resources: The Colorado River, the United States, and Mexico," *Policy Sciences*, vol. 21 (1988), pp. 23–39. Gleick notes that in the 1940s, when the United States and Mexico were negotiating a treaty on water rights, both sides used strong rhetoric. Mexican officials described access to the Colorado River as "a national interest superior to any other," and Californians serving on the treaty committee warned that the treaty would "strike a deadly blow at the country's *national security* by taking water away from southern California's coastal plain—the nation's front on the Pacific" (emphasis added). Since the federal government is obliged to supply a quantity of Colorado water to Mexico, permanent reductions in the river's flow due to climate change could create bilateral problems. See also Peter H. Gleick, "The Implications of Global Climatic Changes for International Security," *Climate Change*, vol. 15 (October 1989), pp. 309–25.

54. As cited in *Environment and Conflict*, Earthscan Briefing Document 40 (Washington, D.C.: Earthscan, November 1984), pp. 22–23.

55. Robert Rotberg, "Haiti's Past Mortgages Its Future, *Foreign Affairs*, vol. 67 (Fall 1988), pp. 97–98.

56. Myers, op. cit., pp. 35–38; *Wall Street Journal*, May 8, 1991; and *New York Times*, May 12, 1991.

57. *World Resources 1990–91*, pp. 254–55; "Too Much Life on Earth?" *New Scientist*, May 19, 1990, p. 28; and Mathews, "Redefining Security," p. 163.
58. *World Resources 1990–91*, pp. 254–55.
59. Taylor, op. cit., 594.
60. Lester Brown, *Redefining National Security*, p. 38.
61. Earthscan, op. cit., p. 7. The U.N. report noted, "In recent years there has been a marked tendency in international relations to use or threaten to use military force in response to nonmilitary challenges to security." The Independent Commission on International Development Issues, chaired by Willy Brandt, reported to the U.N. secretary general in 1980: "Our survival depends not only on military balance but on global cooperation to ensure a sustainable biological environment and sustainable prosperity based on equitably shared resources" (as quoted in Neville Brown, "Climate, Ecology, and International Security," *Survival*, vol. [November/December, 1989], p. 521.) Peter Thatcher, former deputy director of the U.N. Environmental Programme, said in 1982, "The ultimate choice is between conservation or conflict. Trees now or tanks later. The choice for governments is either to find the means by which to pay now to stop the destruction of the natural resource base, or to be prepared to pay later, possibly in blood" (as quoted in Earthscan, op. cit., p. 7).
62. Earthscan, op. cit., p. 14.
63. Ullman, op. cit., p. 149.
64. Hobart Rowen, "Global Overpopulation," *Washington Post*, February 17, 1985.
65. Earthscan, op. cit., pp. 1–83.
66. See, for instance, Joyce Starr and Daniel Stoll, *U.S. Foreign Policy on Water Resources in the Middle East*, (Washington, D.C.: Center for Strategic and International Studies, December 1987); Myers, op. cit.; Hal Harvey, "Natural Security," *Nuclear Times*, March/April 1988, pp. 24–26; A. H. Westing, ed., *Global Resources and International Conflict: Environmental Factors in Strategic Policy and Action* (Oxford: Oxford University Press, 1986); Mathews, "Redefining Security"; Janet Welsh Brown, ed., *In the U.S. Interest: Resources, Growth, and Security in the Developing World* (Boulder, Col.: Westview Press, 1990); and Thomas Homer-Dixon, "On the Threshold: Environmental Changes as Causes of Acute Conflict," *International Security*, vol. 16 (Fall 1991).

67. See, for instance, Gregory Foster et al., "Global Demographic Trends to the Year 2010: Implications for U.S. Security," *Washington Quarterly*, vol. 12 (Spring 1989), pp. 5–24, and Sam Sarkesian, "The Demographic Component of Strategy," *Survival*, vol. 31 (November/December 1989), pp. 549–64.

68. Foster et al., op. cit., p. 25.

69. See, for instance, Neville Brown, op. cit.; Gleick, "Implications of Global Climatic Changes"; and Gareth Porter, op. cit. The 1987 international study *Our Common Future* (Oxford: Oxford University Press, 1987), requested by the U.N. secretary general, observed, "Environmental threats to security are now beginning to emerge on a global scale. The most worrisome of these stem from the possible consequences of global warming caused by the atmospheric build-up of carbon dioxide and other gases" (as quoted in Neville Brown, op. cit., p. 524).

70. National Academy of Sciences, *Policy Implications of Global Warming*, p. 81.

71. Daniel Deudney, "The Case Against Linking Environmental Degradation and National Security," *Millennium: Journal of International Studies*, vol. 19 (Winter 1990), pp. 470–74, and Thomas Homer-Dixon, *Environmental Change and Violent Conflict*, Occasional Paper No. 4, (Cambridge, Mass.: American Academy of Arts and Sciences, June 1990), p. 16.

72. Mubarek quoted in "More Precious than Oil, and Maybe as Volatile," *New York Times*, March 17, 1990. See also Starr, op. cit., p. 19.

73. Philip Shabecoff, "Traditional Definitions of National Security are Shaken by Global Environmental Threats," *New York Times*, May 29, 1989.

74. Michael Renner, *National Security: The Economic and Environmental Dimensions*, Worldwatch Paper No. 89 (Washington, D.C.: Worldwatch Institute, May 1989), p. 63.

75. Deudney, op. cit., pp. 467–68.

76. Eugene B. Skolnikoff, "The Policy Gridlock on Global Warming," *Foreign Policy*, no. 77, (Summer 1990), p. 82.

77. Peter H. Gleick, "Environment and Security: The Clear Connections," *Bulletin of the Atomic Scientists*, April 1991, pp. 17–21.

78. Nazli Choucri, Janet Brown, and Peter Haas in Brown, ed., *In the U.S. Interest*, pp. 93–94.

79. Al Gore, "SEI: A Strategic Environment Initiative," *SAIS Review*, vol. 10 (Winter/Spring 1990), p. 60 (emphasis added).

80. In a very real sense, our national security strategy and budget have always been aimed at *long-term* threats. The doctrine of containment, and the idea of the Cold War, were themselves based on the notion that U.S. national security depended on victory in a long-term struggle with the Soviets. For instance, Secretary of State Dean Acheson said in 1947: "We are in a period now I think of the formulation of mood. The country is getting serious. It is getting impressed by the fact that the business of dealing with the Russians is a long, long job. People . . . now see it as a long, long pull, and that it can only be done by the United States getting itself together, determining that we cannot maintain a counter-balance to the communistic power without strengthening all those other parts of the world which belong in the system with us. That takes money, imagination, American skill and American technical help and many, many years" (Yergin, *Shattered Peace*, p. 5). For most of the Cold War period, we were not faced with imminent attack. Even if the entire nuclear weapons budget was allotted to ensuring the territorial integrity of the United States, it rarely accounted for more than 15 percent of the overall military budget. Most of the military budget went to indirect threats, to containing the Soviet Union, in other words, to longer term threats. Even elements of the nuclear budget were sometimes defended not as being crucial to avoid imminent attack but to maintain the credibility of our deterrent over the longer term. It took us 45 years to win the Cold War struggle with the Soviets, and most were surprised when it happened. It therefore seems incongruous to argue that environmental and economic threats facing the nation are not legitimate security threats merely because they are long-term dangers that require long-term approaches.

81. Maull, op. cit., p. 502.

82. Daniel Yergin, "Energy Security in the 1990s," *Foreign Affairs*, vol. 67 (Fall 1988), p. 111.

83. Daniel Yergin, *The Prize: The Epic Quest for Money, Oil, and Power* (New York: Simon and Schuster, 1991), p. 567.

84. Ibid., p. 662.

85. Schultze, op. cit., p. 529.

86. Taylor, op.cit., pp. 592–93.

87. Quoted in Ralph Cavanagh et al., "National Energy Policy," *World Policy Journal*, vol. 6 (Spring 1989), p. 242.
88. Quoted in Thomas McNaugher, *Arms And Oil* (Washington, D.C.: Brookings Institution, 1985), p. 3.
89. Quoted in Jordan and Taylor, op. cit., p. 287 (emphasis added).
90. The energy statistics are from Arthur H. Rosenfeld, "Energy Options: Technological Solutions and Limits" (Presentation at the University of California, Berkeley, January 23, 1992), and Yergin, "Energy Security in the 1990s," p. 115. The pay-off of federal energy efficiency investments is from Arthur H. Rosenfeld, "The Role of Federal Research and Development in Advancing Energy Efficiency," testimony before the Subcommittee on Environment of the House Committee on Science, Space, and Technology, April 17, 1991. Not all of Carter's energy policies were successful. The Synthetic Fuels Corporation, for example, never produced a single barrel of oil substitutes, despite an investment of $8 billion.
91. Yergin, *The Prize*, 765–66.
92. Quoted in "Bush Says Iraqi Aggression Threatens 'Our Way of Life,'" *New York Times*, August 16, 1990.
93. Interestingly, an April 1990 DOE summary of its public hearings stated: "The loudest single message was to increase energy efficiency in every sector of energy use. Energy efficiency was seen as a way to reduce pollution, reduce dependence on imports, and reduce the cost of energy." The final version of the National Energy Strategy, however, did not reflect this message (*Interim Report, National Energy Strategy: A Compilation of Public Comments*, DOE/S-0066P, April 1990, as quoted in *America's Energy Choices* [Cambridge, Mass.: Union of Concerned Scientists, 1991], pp. 25–26).
94. Few experts believe that the United States can reverse the steady decline in domestic oil production that began in the mid-1980s. See, for instance, Robert K. Kaufmann and Cutler J. Cleveland, "Policies to Increase U.S. Oil Production: Likely to Fail, Damage the Economy, and Damage the Environment," *Annual Review of Energy and the Environment*, vol. 16 (1991), pp. 379–400.
95. U.S. Department of Energy, *National Energy Strategy* (Washington, D.C.: Government Printing Office, February 1991), p. 3 (emphasis in original).
96. M. A. Adelman, "Oil Fallacies," *Foreign Policy* (Winter 1991), p. 12.

97. Ibid., p. 13.
98. James Schlesinger, "Oil and National Security: An American Dilemma," in Edward Fried and Nanette Blandin, eds., *Oil and America's Security* (Washington, D.C.: Brookings Institution, 1988), p. 11.
99. Ibid., p. 13.
100. James Baker, testimony before the House Foreign Relations Committee, February 6, 1991.
101. Office of Technology Assessment, *U.S. Oil Import Vulnerability* (Washington, D.C.: Government Printing Office, October 1991), p. 17, and Christopher Flavin, "Detroit: America's Best Source of Oil," *New York Times*, August 26, 1990.
102. Amory Lovins and L. Hunter Lovins, "Make Fuel Efficiency Our Gulf Strategy," *New York Times*, December 3, 1990.
103. Yergin, "Energy Security in the 1990s," p. 130; Allison and Treverton, op. cit., p. 456.
104. See, for instance, Harold Hubbard, "The Real Cost of Energy," *Scientific American*, April 1991, pp. 36–42; Harvey, op. cit.; and Seymour Deitchman, *After the Cold War: U.S. Security for the Future*, Occasional Paper (Washington, D.C.: Atlantic Council, August 1990).
105. Moran, op. cit., p. 85. He adds, "For those concerned about a 'level playing field' for U.S. competitiveness, an energy tax of up to $2–$3 per gallon of gasoline would simply match the burden borne by Asian and European firms."
106. See, for instance, Ullman, op. cit.
107. Marc Ledbetter and Marc Ross, "Supply Curves of Conserved Energy for Automobiles" (Paper prepared for Lawrence Berkeley Laboratory, Applied Science Division, Berkeley, California, March 1990), and National Academy of Sciences, *Policy Implications of Global Warming*, p. 59. For a different view, see Seymour Deitchman, *Beyond the Thaw: A New National Strategy* (Boulder, Col.: Westview Press, 1991), p. 125. Deitchman, a former Defense Department analyst, estimates a replacement cost of $22 to $29 per barrel, $5 to $10 per barrel *above* 1989 prices. Deitchman nevertheless believes the effort would be worth the cost because of the benefits to U.S. national security of eliminating dependence on Middle East oil, including the possibility of reducing defense spending.
108. Moran, op. cit., p. 83, and Maull, op. cit., p. 506.
109. Edward L. Morse, "The Coming Oil Revolution," *Foreign Affairs*, vol. 69 (Winter 1990/91), p. 37.

110. "Two Big California Utilities Plan to Cut CO_2 Emissions," *New York Times*, May 21, 1991, and EPA Urging Electricity Efficiency," *New York Times*, January 16, 1991. For two recent analyses of possible carbon dioxide reductions, see Amory B. Lovins and L. Hunter Lovins, "Least-Cost Climatic Stabilization" and D. F. Spencer, "A Preliminary Assessment of Carbon Dioxide Mitigation" in *Annual Review of Energy and the Environment*, vol. 16 (1991).

111. Amory B. Lovins et al., *Least-cost Energy: Solving the CO_2 Problem* (Andover, Mass.: Brick House Publishing, 1981).

112. See Carl J. Weinberg and Robert H. Williams, "Energy from the Sun," Arnold P. Fickett et al., "Efficient Use of Electricity," and Rick Bevington and Arthur H. Rosenfeld, "Energy for Buildings and Homes," in Ged Davis et al., *Energy for Planet Earth* (New York: W. H. Freeman, 1991).

113. Arnold P. Fickett, op. cit., p. 15.

114. National Academy of Sciences, *Policy Implications of Global Warming*, p. 75.

115. Bevington and Rosenfeld, op. cit., p. 34.

116. One early study was the American Assembly's *Economic Security for Americans* (Ann Arbor: University Microfilms International, 1954). This report was the product of the discussions of the economists, politicians and civil servants, businessmen, and policy analysts who gathered in 1953 at the third American Assembly Conference. It stated: "The opportunity to work, without interruption and for good wages, is the most valuable form of security for most Americans" (p. 9). Forty years ago, however, economic security meant social security, not competitiveness: The "four major hazards to economic security" discussed were "old age, unemployment, sickness and disability, and possible death of a breadwinner" (p. 17).

117. Rostow, op. cit., p. 191.

118. As quoted in Ralph K. Andrist, ed., *The Founding Fathers, George Washington: A Biography in His Own Words* (New York: *Newsweek*, 1972), p. 372. The address was never actually delivered but was published widely in the 1790s.

119. Maier, op. cit., pp. 10–11.

120. Ernest R. May, "National Security in American History," in Graham Allison and Gregory F. Treverton (eds.), op. cit., pp. 14–15.

121. Quoted in an early draft of Ernest May, "National Security in American History," in Graham Allison and Gregory F. Treverton (eds.), op. cit., pp. 11–12.

122. Melvin P. Leffler (and John Gaddis et al.), "The American Conception of National Security and the Beginnings of the Cold War, 1945 1948," (and Comments), *American Historical Review Forum*, vol. 89 (April 1984), p. 383.

123. Quoted in May, op. cit., pp. 104–105. Eisenhower's formulation of security echoes one put forward by Harold Lasswell in his 1950 work, *National Security and Individual Freedom*, in a chapter titled, "The Meaning of National Security Policy":

> Our security is affected not only by what the citizen thinks of our defense program; it is also affected by the impact of the program upon our physical resources. If we overspend in the name of national defense, we weaken American security. . . . Excessive mobilization of assets for security purposes is in fact an immobilization of resources for all purposes, including security. . . .
>
> Two of the chief points of attack against the United States in foreign countries, for instance, are the alleged inherent instability of our economic system and the prevalence of discrimination against colored peoples. Whatever measures are taken at home to maintain high levels of productive employment and to reduce discrimination also strengthen our position abroad. Security policies are thus being made whenever any decision influences the stability of our economic life or the degree to which opportunity is made to depend upon individual merit.
>
> *The conclusion is that American security measures should be the outcome of a comprehensive process of balancing the costs and benefits of all policies in the foreign and domestic fields.*

The tragic riots in Los Angeles in 1992 suggest the continuing relevance of Lasswell words. Nations we have accused of human rights violations—China, Libya, Iraq—piously accuse us of hypocrisy. But even our allies increasingly see us as a nation that either cannot or will not solve its problems. Keeping our position as world leader will require restoring our economic security.

124. Merlo Pusey, *Eisenhower the President* (New York: MacMillan, 1956), pp. 246–47.

125. Douglas Kinnard, *President Eisenhower and Strategy Management* (Lexington: University Press of Kentucky, 1977), pp. 127, 128, 135.

126. Huddle, quoted in Lester Brown, *Redefining National Security*, p. 41; Schmidt quoted in Jordan and Taylor, op. cit., p. 3.

127. Edwin J. Feulner, Jr., "The Economic Factor in United States National Security Policy," in James Dornan, ed.,

U.S. National Security Policy in the Decade Ahead, (Russak, N.J.: Crane, 1978), p. 32.

128. Quoted in Jordan and Taylor, op. cit., p. 287.

129. Stephen Cohen et al., "Global Competition: The New Reality," *Working Paper of the President's Commission on Industrial Competitiveness*, vol. 3 (1984), as quoted in Michael Borrus and John Zysman, "The Highest Stakes: Industrial Competitiveness and National Security," BRIE Working Paper 39, April 1991, pp. 47–48 (to appear as a chapter in Wayne Sandholtz et al., *The Highest Stakes: Technology, Economy and Security Policy* [New York: Oxford University Press, 1992]). According to the Commission:

> A nation's competitiveness is the degree to which it can, under free and fair market conditions, produce goods and services that meet the test of international markets while simultaneously expanding the real incomes of its citizens. International competitiveness at that national level is based on superior productivity performance and the economy's ability to shift output to high productivity activities, which in turn can generate high levels of real wages. Competitiveness is associated with rising living standards, expanding employment opportunities, and the ability of a nation to maintain its international obligations. It is not just a measure of the nation's ability to sell abroad, and to maintain a trade equilibrium. The very poorest countries in the world are often able to do that quite well. Rather, it is the nation's ability to stay ahead technologically and commercially in those commodities and services likely to constitute a larger share of world consumption and value-added in the future.

130. See Michael Porter, *The Competitive Advantage of Nations* (New York: Free Press, 1990).

131. See, for instance, Robert Reich, *The Work of Nations* (New York: Alfred A. Knopf, 1991), chapter 21, "The Decline of Public Investment." A 1990 study by the Economic Policy Institute concluded that "more than half of the decline in our productivity growth over the the past two decades can be explained by lower public infrastructure spending" (David Alan Aschauer, *Public Investment and Private Sector Growth* [Washington, D.C.: Economic Policy Institute, 1990], p. 1).

132. Quoted in Walter Massey, "Science Education in the United States: What the Scientific Community Can Do," *Science*, September 1, 1989, p. 917. See also Office of Technology Assessment, *Making Things Better: Competing in Manufacturing*, OTA-ITE-443 (Washington, D.C.: Government Printing Office, February 1990), p. 13.

133. Robert Reich, "Who Champions the Working Class?" *New York Times*, May 26, 1991 (the wage comparison is inflation adjusted); Arthur Kennickell and Janice Shack-Marquez, "Changes in Family Finances from 1983 to 1989: Evidence from the Survey of Consumer Finances," *Federal Reserve Bulletin*, January 1992, pp. 1–18; U.S. Bureau of the Census, *Money Income of Households, Families, and Persons in the United States 1990* (Washington, D.C.: Government Printing Office, August 1991), p. 202; and U.S. Bureau of the Census, *Household Wealth and Asset Ownership: 1988* (Washington, D.C.: Government Printing Office, December 1990).

134. Juliet Schor, *The Overworked American* (New York: Basic Books, 1991), p. 81 (emphasis in original). Schor notes that while Europeans have been gaining vacation time, Americans have been losing it. "In the last decade, U.S. workers have gotten *less* paid time off on the order of three and a half fewer days each year of vacation time, holidays, sick pay, and other paid absences" (p. 32). She also calculates that "leisure time has fallen by 47 hours a year" (p. 36).

135. "Families on a Treadmill: Work and Income in the 1980s," Staff Study for the Joint Economic Committee, U.S. Congress, January 17, 1992, p. 18. Increased expenses created by a second wage-earner include clothing, transportation, and day care. The Economic Policy Institute reported in 1991 that "all of the increase in incomes of married couples with children since 1979 has been contributed by working mothers" (Lawrence Mishel and David M. Frankel, *The State of Working America 1990–91* [Armonk, N.Y.: M. E. Sharpe, 1991], p. xi).

136. In 1988, the average weekly American wage for retail trade was $184; for services, $290; for finance, insurance and real estate, $326; and for manufacturing, $418 (William Serrin, "A Great American Job Machine?" *The Nation*, September 18, 1989, p. 270). The job loss figures are from "Industry Analytical Ratios for Manufacturing," Bureau of Labor Statistics, September 1991. There are now fewer manufacturing jobs than there were in 1967. In the late 1960s, manufacturing workers made up more than 25 percent of the labor force, a figure which dropped to 20 percent by the late 1970s and then plunged to roughly 15 percent by the early 1990s. The vast majority of manufacturing jobs lost since 1979 were in the very high-paying durable goods sector, which makes cars and other long-lasting products.

137. Mishel and Frankel, op. cit., pp. 258–59. During that decade, the hourly compensation of American production workers dropped 0.41 percent per year. The wages of production workers in Japan, France, and West Germany grew every year by 0.92 percent, 2.15 percent, and 1.89 percent, respectively. See also Serrin, "A Great American Job Machine?"

138. Council on Competitiveness, *Gaining New Ground: Technology Priorities for America's Future* (Washington, D.C., 1991). The Council on Competitiveness is a nonprofit, nonpartisan organization of leaders from business, higher education, and organized labor working toward improving the competitiveness of American companies and workers. It has no connection with the White House Council on Competitiveness, chaired by Vice President Dan Quayle.

139. *Making Things Better*, p. 3.

140. "The U.S. Achilles' Heel in Desert Storm," *Washington Post National Weekly Edition*, April 1–7, 1991, p. 11, and *60 Minutes*, April 21, 1991.

141. These statistics are from U.S. General Accounting Office, "International Trade," GAO/NSIAD-91-278 (Washington, D.C., September 1991), p. 9; "The Big Split," *Fortune*, May 6, 1991, pp. 41–42; "Computers: Japan Comes on Strong," *Business Week*, October 23, 1989, p. 104; and *Making Things Better*, p. 16.

142. See "Cranking Up the Export Machine," *U.S. News & World Report*, November 18, 1991, p. 78 and "Why Japan's Surplus Is Rising," *Fortune*, December 30, 1991, p. 95.

143. *The Economist*, June 22, 1991, p. 35. On May 8, 1992, Kenneth Courtis, first vice president of Deutsche Bank Capital Markets, Asia, told the Congressional Joint Economic Committee, "I believe that [Japan] will come out of this recession even stronger than it's been in the past. . . . If you take the figures the IMF [International Monetary Fund] released two weeks ago about long-term sustainable growth rates . . . by early in the next decade, the economy of the United States and the economy of Japan would be about the same size. . . . On the basis of investments that have already been made, by the mid-1990s, Japan will have a manufacturing base that's larger than that of the United States."

144. Theodore C. Sorensen, "Rethinking National Security," *Foreign Affairs*, vol. 69 (Summer 1990), pp. 1–18.

145. Edward Luttwak, "From Geopolitics to Geo-Economics," *The National Interest* (Summer 1990), pp. 17–23. Luttwak

holds the Burke Chair in Strategy at the Center for Strategic and International Studies in Washington, D.C.

146. Joseph S. Nye, Jr., *Bound to Lead: The Changing Nature of American Power* (New York: Basic Books, 1990), pp. 179, 228.

147. C. Fred Bergsten, "The World Economy After the Cold War," *Foreign Affairs*, vol. 69 (Summer 1990), pp. 96–112. Bergsten is currently director of the Institute for International Affairs.

148. Ibid., pp. 97–98.

149. Ibid, p. 105.

150. Samuel P. Huntington, "The U.S.—Decline or Renewal?" *Foreign Affairs*, vol. 67 (Winter 1988/89), pp. 84, 92. The first quote, in full, is "In short, if 'hegemony' means having 40 percent or more of world economic activity (a percentage Britain never remotely approximated during its hegemonic years), American hegemony disappeared long ago. If hegemony means producing 20 to 25 percent of the world product and twice as much as any other individual country, American hegemony looks quite secure." Nye cites this passage in *Bound to Lead*, p. 72.

151. Samuel P. Huntington, "America's Changing Strategic Interests," *Survival*, vol. 33 (January/February 1991), p. 16.

152. Ibid., pp. 5–9.

153. Ibid., p. 10.

154. Ibid., p. 13.

155. Michael Porter, op.cit., pp. 723–24. Similarly, Michael Dertouzos, head of the department of computer sciences at the Massachusetts Institute of Technology, said the United States is in a "manufacturing war. . . . We're going to wind up with a reduced standard of living. . . . We're going to be impoverished relative to other nations in terms of our standard of living if we don't wake up and address these issues" (*60 Minutes*, April 21, 1991).

156. Huntington, "America's Changing Strategic Interests," p. 15.

157. Deitchman, *After the Cold War*, pp. 31, 37. For another comprehensive budget for dealing with America's post Cold War problems, see Richard J. Barnet et al., "American Priorities in a New World Era," *World Policy Journal*, vol. 6 (Spring 1989), pp. 203–37.

158. B. R. Inman and Daniel F. Burton, Jr., "Technology and Competitiveness: The New Policy Frontier," *Foreign Affairs*, vol. 69 (Spring 1990) pp. 123, 124, 133.

159. Quoted in Robert Kuttner, *The End of Laissez-Faire: National Purpose and the Global Economy After the Cold War* (New York: Alfred A. Knopf, 1991), p. 222.
160. Harold Brown, "The United States and Japan: High Tech Is Foreign Policy," *SAIS Review*, Summer/Fall 1989, pp. 13–14.
161. Kuttner, op. cit., p. 194.
162. See, for instance, Selig S. Harrison and Clyde V. Prestowitz, Jr., "Pacific Agenda: Defense or Economics?" *Foreign Policy* (Summer 1990); Clyde V. Prestowitz, Jr., *Trading Places: How We Allowed Japan to Take the Lead* (New York: Basic Books, 1988), chapter 8, "Traders or Warriors: The Conflict Between Economic and National Security"; and Council on Competitiveness, *Gaining New Ground*. See also, *Finding Common Ground* (1991) and *Balancing the National Interest* (1987), both published by the National Academy of Sciences.
163. Kuttner, op. cit., p. 227.
164. Harold H. Brown, op. cit., p. 15.
165. Nye, op. cit., p. 250. Joseph Fitchett writes, "In the United States, where ball-bearing makers recently tried to get protection from foreign competition, calls to safeguard a national "defense-industrial base" often are simply codes for non-tariff barriers, and the national security umbrella increasingly shelters protectionism and services" (*International Herald Tribune*, December 16, 1988, as quoted in Miles Wolpin, American Insecurity (Jefferson, N.C.: McFarland, 1991), p. 3.
166. As cited in Kuttner, op. cit., p. 223.
167. Ishihara quoted in "A Japan That Can Take Credit," *Newsweek*, July 15, 1991, p. 27; David Gergen, "America as Techno-Colony," *U.S. News and World Report*, April 1, 1991, p. 88.
168. Moran, op. cit., pp. 80–82. Moran develops this analysis at greater length in "The Globalization of America's Defense Industries: Managing the Threat of Foreign Dependence," *International Security* (Summer 1990), pp. 57–100.
169. "Industrial Policy," *Business Week*, April 6, 1992, pp. 70–76, and Joseph Romm, "The Gospel According to Sun Tzu," *Forbes*, December 11, 1991, pp. 154–62. The *Business Week* article was a cover story announcing the magazine's support for an industrial policy, which it detailed inside. According to the *Forbes* article, "The reason America is having trouble competing economically is that we . . . neither invest in a highly trained work force, nor

devote adequate resources to advanced civilian technology, nor take a systematic approach to our economic strategy, such as having a fast-cycle production system or a manufacturing industrial policy."

170. "White House Lists 22 Critical Technologies," *New York Times*, April 26, 1991. See also "Report of the National Critical Technologies Panel," Washington, D.C.: The White House, March 1991.

171. For discussion of Japanese "unfair" trading practices, see Edward J. Lincoln, *Japan's Unequal Trade* (Washington, D.C.: Brookings Institution, 1990); Prestowitz, *Trading Places*; and Karel von Wolferen, "The Japan Problem Revisited," *Foreign Affairs*, vol. 69 (Fall 1990), pp. 42–55. For an alternative view, see, for instance, Philip Trezise, "Japan, the Enemy?" *The Brookings Review*, vol. 8 (Winter 1989/90), pp. 3–13, and Yoshi Tsurumi, "U.S.–Japanese Relations: From Brinkmanship to Statesmanship," *World Policy Journal* (Winter 1989 90), pp. 1–33.

172. "The Yen Block," *Economist*, July 15, 1989, p. 6; Harold Brown, op. cit., p. 11; and Harrison and Prestowitz, op. cit., pp. 61–62. Harrison is a former Northeast Asia bureau chief for the *Washington Post*. Prestowitz is a former U.S. trade negotiator.

173. J. W. M. Chapman et al., *Japan's Quest for Comprehensive Security* (New York: St. Martin's Press, 1982), p. 149.

174. Norman D. Levin, "Japan's Defense Policy: The Internal Debate," in Harry Kendall and Clara Joewono, eds., *Japan, ASEAN, and the United States*, (Berkeley: Institute of East Asian Studies, University of California, 1991), p. 84. See also Umemoto Tetsuya, "Comprehensive Security and the Evolution of the Japanese Security Posture," in Robert Scalapino et al., eds., *Asian Security Issues*, (Berkeley: Institute of East Asian Studies, University of California, 1988), pp. 32–38.

175. I have eliminated the phrase "under free and fair market conditions" from the earlier definition of security. While the real incomes of a nation's citizens can be measured relatively unambiguously, "free and fair market conditions" is undefined, and may be undefinable, since, at the very least, individual nations are likely to disagree about what such conditions are.

176. Supporting the less fortunate has traditionally been a central component of U.S. economic security. As noted earlier, the "four major hazards to economic security" considered by the 1953 American Assembly conference were "old age,

unemployment, sickness and disability, and possible death of a breadwinner." See *Economic Security for Americans*, p. 17.

177. In America, the income of the richest fifth of the population was 8.9 times the income of the poorest fifth over the period 1980 to 1987. In France, that ratio was 6.5, in Germany it was 5.7, and in Japan it was 4.3. Michael Kidron and Ronald Segal, *The New State of the World Atlas*, 4th ed. (New York: Simon & Schuster, 1991), p. 36. Income distribution in the United States has become more *inequitable* in recent years. In 1989, for instance, the ratio was 9.7. In contrast, in the late 1960s and early 1970s, income distribution was more equitable and the ratio was about 7.4. See Mishel and Frankel, op. cit., p. 20.

178. Lasswell, op. cit., p. 51 (emphasis in original).

179. I have eliminated the reference to "private nongovernmental entities" primarily to highlight the distinction between the two components economic security and economic independence.

180. As Ullman has argued (op. cit., pp. 133–34), the threat posed by the Soviet Union was not put forth principally as one of direct attack on America with drastic degradation in our quality of life (except in the case of nuclear war). Rather, the threat was more that the Soviets would assert domination over Western Europe or other countries that shared our values, substantially closing those societies to us. That is also how the threat to the United States from Nazi Germany was discussed in the years before our entry into World War II. The result of Soviet domination of Europe would have been, in Ullman's words, "fewer opportunities for American traders and investors . . . [and] for unfettered intellectual, cultural, and scientific exchange." The subordination of civil and political liberties in those countries "would have made it more difficult to assure their preservation in an isolated and even besieged United States." Therefore, in a variety of ways, "the range of options open to the United States government, and to persons and groups within American society, would have been importantly diminished."

181. Quoted in Yergin, *Shattered Peace* (1977), p. 5.

182. George Orwell, "Politics and the English Language," in *The Orwell Reader* (New York: Harcourt Brace and Jovanavitch, 1956), pp. 355–66.

183. As cited in Francis Fukuyama, "The End of History?" *The National Interest*, Summer 1989, p. 17.

184. In this formulation, global climate change is seen as the most significant "sustainability" issue for the United States, since our rate of carbon dioxide use (5 percent of the world's population producing 25 percent of the world's carbon dioxide) is clearly not one that can be sustainably adopted by the rest of the world. Other countries, with far fewer natural resources, have more basic sustainability concerns relating to water, soil, forests, and population growth.

185. See Joseph J. Romm, *The Once and Future Superpower* (New York: William Morrow, 1992), especially chapter five, "Environmental Security and the Industrial Ecosystem."

186. As cited in John E. Gray et al., "Global Climate Change: U.S. Japan Cooperative Leadership for Environmental Protection," Occasional Paper, (Washington, D.C.: Atlantic Council, November 1991), p. 68. See also "Action Program to Arrest Global Warming," Decision made by the Council of Ministers for Global Environment Conservation, Government of Japan, October 23, 1990, p. 14, and "Can Japan Put the Brakes on Global Warming?" *Scientific American*, August 1991, p. 98. MITI has established the Research Institute for Innovative Technology for the Earth to develop environmental technologies.

187. Nobutoshi Akao, *Japan's Economic Security* (New York: Royal Institute for International Affairs, 1983), p. 1, as cited in George Friedman and Meredith LeBard, *The Coming War with Japan* (New York: St. Martin's Press, 1991), p. 9.

188. Robert Reich poses an interesting dilemma in his public lectures. Over the next ten years, he asks, would you rather have the U.S. economy grow by 25 percent and Japan's economy by 75 percent or the U.S. economy grow by 8.3 percent and Japan's economy by 8.4 percent? His audiences often chose the second option, even though it condemns the United States to a decade of economic stagnation. It appears that those who choose the second option view Japan as the enemy.

189. Taylor, op. cit., p. 594; Nye, op. cit., p. 227; Council on Competitiveness, *Gaining New Ground*, p. 49; and Huntington, "America's Changing Strategic Interests," p. 15.

Bibliography

National Security:
General and Historical

Graham Allison and Gregory Treverton, eds., *Rethinking America's Security* (New York: Norton, 1992).

Richard J. Barnet et al, "American Priorities in a New World Era," *World Policy Journal*, Vol. VI, No. 2 (Spring 1989), pp. 203–37.

Morton Berkowitz and P. G. Bock, "National Security," Vol. 11, in David L. Sills (ed.), *International Encyclopedia of the Social Sciences* (New York: MacMillan, 1968), pp. 40–45.

Bernard Brodie, *War and Politics* (New York: MacMillan, 1973).

Lester Brown, *Redefining National Security*, Washington, D.C.: Worldwatch Paper #14, October 1977.

Barry Buzan, *People, States, and Fear: The National Security Problem in International Relations* (Chapel Hill: University of North Carolina Press, 1983).

Harlan Cleveland and Stuart Gerry Brown, "The Limits of Obsession: Fencing in the 'National Security' Claim," *Administrative Law Review*, Vol. 28, No. 3 (Summer 1976), pp. 327–46.

Herman E. Daly and John B. Cobb, Jr., *For the Common Good* (Boston: Beacon Press, 1989).

Seymour Deitchman, *After the Cold War: U.S. Security for the Future*, Occasional Paper, Washington, D.C.: Atlantic Council, August 1990.

Seymour Deitchman, *Beyond the Thaw: A New National Strategy* (Boulder, Colo.: Westview Press, 1991).

Albert O. Hirschman, *National Power and the Structure*

of Foreign Trade (Berkeley, Ca.: University of California Press, 1945, expanded edition, 1980).

Amos A. Jordan and William J. Taylor, Jr., *American National Security* (Baltimore: Johns Hopkins University Press, 1981).

Douglas Kinnard, *President Eisenhower and Strategy Management* (Lexington: The University Press of Kentucky, 1977).

Harold D. Lasswell, *National Security and Individual Freedom* (New York: McGraw-Hill, 1950), pp. 50–75.

Melvin P. Leffler (and John Gaddis et al), "The American Conception of National Security and the Beginnings of the Cold War, 1945–1948," (and Comments), *American Historical Review Forum*, Vol. 89, No. 2 (April, 1984), pp. 346–99.

Charles Maier, "Peace and Security Studies for the 1990s," unpublished paper for MacArthur SSRC Fellowship Program, June 12, 1990.

Ernest May, "National Security in American History," chapter three of Graham Allison and Gregory Treverton, eds., *Rethinking America's Security* (New York: Norton, 1992), pp. 94–114.

Richard H. Moss and Richard C. Rockwell, "Reconceptualizing Security: A Note about Research," in Sergio Aguayo Quezado and Bruce M. Bagley eds., *Issues in Mexican National Security* (Mexico City: Siglo Veintiuno Editores, 1990)

Robert Post, "National Security and the Amended Freedom of Information Act," *Yale Law Journal*, Vol. 85 (January 1976), pp. 401–22.

Joseph J. Romm, *The Once and Future Superpower: How to Restore America's Economic, Energy, and Environmental Security* (New York: William Morrow, 1992).

Charles Schultze, "The Economic Content of National Security Policy," *Foreign Affairs*, April 1973, pp. 522–40.

Maxwell D. Taylor, "The Legitimate Claims of National Security," *Foreign Affairs*, Vol. 52, No. 3 (April 1974), pp. 577–94.

Richard Ullman, "Redefining Security," *International Security*, Vol. 8, No. 1 (Summer 1983), pp. 129–53.

Arnold Wolfers, Discord and Collaboration (Baltimore: The Johns Hopkins University Press, 1962), pp. 147–65.

Miles Wolpin, *America Insecure: Arms Transfers, Global Interventionism, and the Erosion of National Security* (Jefferson, N.C.: McFarland & Company, 1991), pp. 1–7.

Adam Yarmolinsky, *The Military Establishment* (New York: Harper and Row, 1971), pp. 93–95.

Daniel Yergin, *Shattered Peace: The Origins of the Cold War and the National Security State* (Boston: Houghton Mifflin, 1977).

Drug Policy and National Security

Bruce M. Bagley, "Dateline Drug Wars: Columbia: The Wrong Strategy," *Foreign Policy*, 77 (Winter 1989/90), pp. 154–71.

Bruce Bagley, "The New Hundred Years War? U.S. National Security and the War on Drugs in Latin America," *Journal of Interamerican Studies and World Affairs*, Vol. 30, No. 1, Spring 1988.

Michael J. Dziedzic, "The Transnational Drug Trade and Regional Security," *Survival*, Vol. 31, No. 6 (November/December, 1989), pp. 533–48.

Michael T. Klare, "Fighting Drugs with the Military," *The Nation*, January 1, 1990, pp. 8–12.

Donald Mabry, "The U.S. Military and the War on Drugs in Latin America," *Journal of Interamerican Studies and World Affairs*, Summer/Fall 1988.

Scott B. MacDonald, "Slaying the Drug Hydra," *SAIS Review*, Winter-Spring, 1989.

Waltraud Q. Morales, "The War on Drugs: A New National Security Doctrine?" *Third World Quarterly*, Vol. 11, No. 3 (July 1989), pp. 147–69.

Raphael F. Perl, "United States International Drug Policy: Recent Developments and Issues," *Journal of Interamerican Studies and World Affairs*, Vol. 32, No. 4, (Winter 1990), pp. 123–35.

Juan G. Tokatlian, "National Security and Drugs: Their Impact on Colombian–U.S. Relations," in *Journal of Interamerican Studies and World Affairs*, Vol. 30, No. 1 (Spring 1988), pp. 133–60.

Environmental Security

Richard Benedick et al., *Greenhouse Warming: Negotiating a Global Regime*, Washington, D.C.: World Resources Institute, January 1991.

Janet Welsh Brown, ed., *In the U.S. Interest: Resources, Growth, and Security in the Developing World* (Boulder, Colo.: Westview Press, 1990).

Lester Brown, *Redefining National Security*, Washington, D.C.: Worldwatch Paper No. 14, October 1977.

Neville Brown, "Climate, Ecology, and International Security," *Survival*, Vol. XXXI, No. 6 (November/December, 1989), pp. 519–32.

Congressional Research Service Interdivisional Team, coordinated by Martin Lee, "Applying Defense Resources to Environmental Problems," CRS Issue Brief 90127, Washington, D.C.: CRS, February 5, 1991.

Congressional Research Service, "The Environment as a Foreign Policy Issue," (by Curt Tarnoff), Washington, D.C.: CRS, June 3, 1991.

Daniel Deudney, "The Case Against Linking Environmental Degradation and National Security," *Millennium: Journal of International Studies*, Vol. 19, No. 3 (Winter 1990), pp. 461–76.

Daniel Deudney, "Environment and Security: Muddled Thinking," *The Bulletin of the Atomic Scientists*, April 1991, pp. 22–28.

Earthscan, Environment and Conflict, Earthscan briefing document 40, Washington, D.C.: November 1984.

Nicholas Eberstadt, "Population Change and National Security," *Foreign Affairs*, Vol. 70, No. 3, (Summer 1991), pp. 115–31.

Gregory Foster et al., "Global Demographic Trends to the Year 2010: Implications for U.S. Security," The

Washington Quarterly, Vol. 12, No. 2 (Spring 1989), pp. 5–24.

Peter H. Gleick, "The Effects of Future Climatic Changes on International Water Resources: the Colorado River, the United States, and Mexico," *Policy Sciences*, Vol. 21 (1988), pp. 23–39.

Peter Gleick, "Environment and Security: The Clear Connections," *The Bulletin of the Atomic Scientists*, April 1991, pp. 17–21.

Peter Gleick, "The Implications of Global Climatic Changes for International Security," *Climate Change*, Vol. 15, no. 1/2 (October 1989), pp. 309–25.

John Glenn, "National Security: More Than Just Weapons Production," *Issues in Science and Technology*, Vol. V, No. 4 (Summer 1989), pp. 27–28.

Al Gore, "SEI: A Strategic Environment Initiative," SAIS Review, Vol. 10, No. 1 (Winter/Spring 1990), pp. 59–71.

Hal Harvey, "Natural Security," *Nuclear Times*, March/April 1988, pp. 24–26.

Sara Hoagland and Susan Conbere, *Environmental Stress and National Security* (College Park: Center for Global Change, University of Maryland, 1991).

Thomas Homer-Dixon, *Environmental Change and Violent Conflict*, Occasional Paper No. 4, Cambridge, Mass.: American Academy of Arts and Sciences, June 1990.

Thomas Homer-Dixon, "On the Threshold: Environmental Changes as Causes of Acute Conflict," *International Security*, Vol. 16, No. 2 (Fall 1991), pp. 76–116.

Ronnie Lipschutz and John Holdren, "Crossing Borders: Resource Flows, the Global Environment, and International Security," Resources and Security Working Paper No. 1 (Berkeley, Cal.: Pacific Institute for Studies in Development, Environment, and Security, March 1989).

Jessica Tuchman Mathews, "The Environment and International Security," in Michael Klare and Daniel Thomas, eds., *World Security*, (New York: St. Martin's Press, 1991), pp. 362–80.

Jessica Tuchman Mathews, "Redefining Security," *Foreign Affairs*, Vol. 68, No. 2 (Spring 1989), pp. 162–77.

National Academy of Sciences, *Policy Implications of Greenhouse Warming* (Washington, D.C.: National Academy Press, 1991).

Norman Myers, "Environment and Security," *Foreign Policy*, Spring 1989, pp. 23–41.

Gareth Porter, "Post–Cold War Global Environment and Security," *The Fletcher Forum*, Summer 1990, pp. 332–44.

Gwyn Prins and Robbie Stamp, *Top Guns & Toxic Whales: The Environment & Global Security* (London: Earthscan Publications Ltd, 1991).

Michael Renner, "Assessing the Military's War on the Environment," in Lester Brown et al., *The State of the World 1991* (New York: Norton, 1991), pp. 132–52.

Michael Renner, *National Security: The Economic and Environmental Dimensions*, Worldwatch Paper No. 89. Washington, D.C.: Worldwatch Institute, May 1989.

Sam Sarkesian, "The demographic component of strategy," *Survival*, Vol. XXXI, No. 6 (November/December 1989), pp. 549–64.

Eugene B. Skolnikoff, "The Policy Gridlock on Global Warming," *Foreign Policy*, No. 77, Summer 1990, pp. 77–93.

Joyce Starr, "Water Wars," *Foreign Policy*, Winter 1991, pp. 17–36.

Joyce Starr and Daniel Stoll, *U.S. Foreign Policy on Water Resources in the Middle East*, Washington, D.C.: CSIS, December 1987.

A. H. Westing, ed., *Cultural Norms, War and the Environment* (Oxford: Oxford University Press, 1988).

A. H. Westing, "The Environmental Component of Comprehensive Security," *Bulletin of Peace Proposals*, Vol. 20, No. 3 (1989), pp. 129–34.

A. H. Westing, ed., *Global Resources and International Conflict: Environmental Factors in Strategic Policy and Action* (Oxford: Oxford University Press, 1986).

Energy Security

M. A. Adelman, "Oil Fallacies," *Foreign Policy*, Winter 1991, pp. 3–16.

Ralph Cavanagh et al., "National Energy Policy," *World Policy Journal*, Vol. VI., No. 2 (Spring 1989), pp. 239–264.

Ged Davis et al., *Energy for Planet Earth* (New York: W. H. Freeman & Co., 1991).

Department of Energy, *National Energy Strategy* (Washington, D.C.: U.S. Government Printing Office, February 1991).

Edward Fried and Nanette Blandin, eds., *Oil and America's Security*, Washington, D.C.: Brookings Institution, 1988.

Harold Hubbard, "The Real Cost of Energy," *Scientific American*, April 1991, pp. 36–42.

Robert K. Kaufmann and Cutler J. Cleveland, "Policies to Increase U.S. Oil Production: Likely to Fail, Damage the Economy, and Damage the Environment," *Annual Review of Energy and the Environment*, Vol. 16 (1991), pp. 379–400.

Edward Krapels, "Revitalizing U.S. Oil Security Policy," *SAIS Review*, Summer/Fall 1989, pp. 185–201.

Amory B. Lovins and L. Hunter Lovins, "The Avoidable Oil Crisis," *Atlantic Monthly*, December 1987, pp. 22–25.

Amory B. Lovins et al., *Least-cost Energy: Solving the CO_2 Problem* (Andover, Mass.: Brick House Publishing, 1981).

Hanns Maull, "Energy and Resources: the Strategic Dimensions," *Survival*, Vol. XXXI, No. 6 (November/December, 1989), pp. 500–18.

Hanns Maull, "Oil and Influence: The Oil Weapon Examined," in Gregory F. Treverton, ed., *Energy and Security* (London: International Institute for Strategic Studies), 1980, pp. 3–39.

Edward L. Morse, "The Coming Oil Revolution," *Foreign Affairs*, Vol. 69, No. 5 (Winter 1990/91), pp. 36–56.

Office of Technology Assessment, *U.S. Oil Import Vulnerability: The Technical Replacement Capability*, (Washington, D.C.: U.S. Government Printing Office, October, 1991).

Joseph Romm, "Needed—A No-Regrets Energy Policy," *The Bulletin of the Atomic Scientists*, July–August, 1991, pp. 31–36.

James R. Schlesinger, "Oil and National Security: An American Dilemma," in Edward Fried and Nanette Blandin, eds., *Oil and America's Security*, Washington, D.C.: Brookings Institution, 1988.

Irwin Stelzer, "OPEC Specter Looms Large," Issue Paper for the American Enterprise Institute, Washington, D.C., 1990.

Michael A. Toman, "What Do We Know About Energy Security?" *Resources*, No. 101 (Fall 1990), Resources for the Future, Washington, D.C., pp. 1–5.

Daniel Yergin, "Energy Security in the 1990s," *Foreign Affairs*, Vol. 67, No. 1 (Fall 1988), pp. 110–32.

Daniel Yergin, *The Prize* (New York: Simon and Schuster, 1991).

Economic Security

American Assembly, *Economic Security for Americans* (Ann Arbor, Mich.: University Microfilms International, 1954).

Richard Barnet et al., "American Priorities in a New World Era," *World Policy Journal*, Spring 1989, pp. 203–37.

C. Fred Bergsten, "The World Economy After the Cold War," *Foreign Affairs*, Vol. 69, No. 3 (Summer 1990), pp. 96–112.

Richard Best, Jr., "The U.S. Intelligence Community: A Role in Supporting Economic Competitiveness?" CRS Report for Congress (90-571 F), December 7, 1990.

Michael Borrus and John Zysman, "The Highest Stakes: Industrial Competitiveness and National Security,"

BRIE Working Paper 39, April 1991 (to appear as a chapter in Wayne Sandholtz et al., *The Highest Stakes: Technology, Economy and Security Policy*, New York: Oxford University Press, 1992).

David Brock, "The Theory and Practice of Japan-Bashing," *The National Interest*, Fall 1989, pp. 29–40.

Harold Brown, "The United States and Japan: High Tech is Foreign Policy," *SAIS Review*, Summer/Fall 1989, pp. 1–18.

J. W. M. Chapman et al., *Japan's Quest for Comprehensive Security* (New York: St. Martin's Press, 1982).

Stephen S. Cohen and John Zysman, *Manufacturing Matters* (New York: Basic Books, 1987).

Council on Competitiveness, *Gaining New Ground: Technology Priorities for America's Future*, Washington, D.C., 1991.

William S. Dietrich, *In the Shadow of the Rising Sun* (University Park, Penn.: Pennsylvania State University Press, 1991).

Edwin J. Feulner, Jr., "The Economic Factor in United States National Security Policy," in James Dornan, ed., *U.S. National Security Policy in the Decade Ahead*, (Russak, N.J.: Crane, 1978), pp. 31–47.

George Friedman and Meredith LeBard, *The Coming War with Japan* (New York: St. Martin's Press, 1991).

Selig S. Harrison and Clyde V. Prestowitz, Jr., "Pacific Agenda: Defense or Economics?" *Foreign Policy*, Summer 1990, pp. 56–76.

Samuel Huntington, "America's Changing Strategic Interests," *Survival*, Vol. XXXIII, No. 1, (January/February 1991), pp. 3–17.

Samuel Huntington, "The U.S.—Decline or Renewal," *Foreign Affairs*, Vol. 67, No. 2 (Winter 1988/89), pp. 76–96.

B. R. Inman and Daniel F. Burton, Jr., "Technology and Competitiveness: The New Policy Frontier," *Foreign Affairs*, Vol. 69, No. 2 (Spring 1990), pp. 116–34.

Paul Kennedy, *The Rise and Fall of the Great Powers* (New York: Random House, 1987).

Robert Kuttner, *The End of Laissez-Faire: National Purpose and the Global Economy After the Cold War* (New York: Alfred A. Knopf, 1991).

Edward J. Lincoln, *Japan's Unequal Trade* (Washington, D.C.: The Brookings Institution, 1990).

Edward Luttwak, "From Geopolitics to Geo-Economics," *The National Interest*, Summer 1990, pp. 17–23.

Theodore H. Moran, "International Economics and National Security," *Foreign Affairs*, Vol. 69, No. 5 (Winter 1990/91), pp. 74–90.

Joseph S. Nye, Jr., *Bound to Lead: The Changing Nature of American Power* (New York: Basic Books, Inc., 1990).

Clyde V. Prestowitz, Jr., *Trading Places: How We Allowed Japan to Take the Lead* (New York: Basic Books, Inc., 1988).

Charles Schultze, "The Economic Content of National Security Policy," *Foreign Affairs*, Vol. 51, No. 3 (April 1973), pp. 522–40.

Ishihara Shintaro, "Learning to Say No to America," *Japan Echo*, Vol. XVII, No. 1 (Spring 1990), pp. 29–35.

Theodore C. Sorensen, "Rethinking National Security," *Foreign Affairs*, Vol. 69, No. 3 (Summer 1990), pp. 1–18

Paula Stern and Paul London, "A Reexamination of U.S. Trade Policy," *The Washington Quarterly*, Autumn 1988, pp. 55–71.

Umemoto Tetsuya, "Comprehensive Security and the Evolution of the Japanese Security Posture," in Robert Scalapino et al., eds., *Asian Security Issues* (Berkeley: Institute of East Asian Studies, University of California, Berkeley, 1988), pp. 28–49.

Philip Trezise, "Japan, the Enemy?" *The Brookings Review*, Vol. 8, No. 1 (Winter 1989/90), pp. 3–13.

Yoshi Tsurumi, "U.S.–Japanese Relations: From Brinkmanship to Statesmanship," *World Policy Journal*, Winter 1989–90, pp. 1–33.

Karel von Wolferen, "The Japan Problem Revisited," *Foreign Affairs*, Vol. 69, No. 4 (Fall 1990), pp. 42–55.

About the Author

Joseph Romm, a research scholar at Rocky Mountain Institute, Snowmass, Colorado, is the author of *The Once and Future Superpower: How to Restore America's Economic, Energy, and Environmental Security* (William Morrow, 1992). He holds a Ph.D. in physics from M.I.T. In 1987, he won an American Physical Society Congressional Science Fellowship. From 1988 to 1990 he was the President's assistant on international security at the Rockefeller Foundation. In 1990 and 1991, he was adjunct assistant professor at Columbia University's School of International and Public Affairs. He has lectured and written widely on military, energy, environmental, and economic issues. His articles have appeared in *Forbes, The Washington Post, The Los Angeles Times, Scientific American, Technology Review*, and *Foreign Affairs*.

Dr. Romm's most recent work is *Lean and Clean Production: How Businesses Can Increase Competiveness While Reducing Pollution*, a report to the U.S. Environmental Protection Agency and Small Business Administration.